TOMMY
TYNAN

TOMMY TYNAN

RYAN DANES

THE ORIGINAL 'FOOTBALL IDOL'

DB PUBLISHING

First published in Great Britain in 2009 by The Breedon Books Publishing Company Limited, 3 The Parker Centre, Derby, DE21 4SZ.

This paperback edition published in Great Britain in 2014 by DB Publishing, an imprint of JMD Media Ltd

Dedication:
This book is dedicated to my mother, Kathryn.

With thanks to:
John Aldridge, Rick Cowdery, Andrew Taylor, Mike Curnow, Ollie Hayne, The Image Bank, Chris Robinson, Mark Smith (Sheffield Wednesday), Len Ashhurst, Sophie, Lucy & Herman, and the Maddicks.

ISBN 978-1-78091-410-7

Printed and bound in the UK by Copytech (UK) Ltd Peterborough

Contents

Foreword

by John Aldridge

Me and Tommy have a lot of things in common. Fellow Scousers and 'Reds', we both enjoyed our first real successes playing up front together at Newport County – and we could both score goals for fun – in fact, little else mattered to either of us when we were on that pitch! And, yes, we could both be greedy so-and-sos too – especially Tommy!

Tommy was an excellent player. He must have had the edge on me when we were younger as we both had trials with Liverpool and they took him on but left it 14 years before they invited me back! And it cost them £750,000 for the privilege!

It was April 1979 before I was offered my first professional contract by Newport County, who were then in the old Fourth Division. Tommy had already signed for them in the February for a club record fee and it was going to take a lot to displace either him or the outstanding Howard Goddard up front. Sadly, Howard broke his leg early the next season and his misfortune gave me my opportunity to form a partnership with Tommy that the club, I am proud to say, considers to be their best ever, and certainly for the next couple of seasons our partnership was regarded as probably the strongest in the lower Leagues. Tommy's style was perfect for me – we had the right chemistry – and it brought us immediate success with a promotion and Welsh Cup double in our first full season together.

In my first 11 games we both scored six goals and in the next match, a 5–0 win at Stockport, I scored my first League hat-trick. That is a memorable occasion for any player, but what stood out for me that day was Tommy's performance. His movement off the ball got me my goals – and I knew he was hurting after the match because he had not scored himself!

The following season we reached the quarter-final of the European Cup-Winners' Cup against the East German giants Carl Zeiss Jena. I was absolutely gutted to miss those games, but Tommy wrote his name into Welsh football history with both goals in the first leg 2–2 draw in Jena – his second with virtually the last kick of the game. The opposition were packed with internationals but there was no denying him.

That Cup run gave Tommy, for a brief time, the sort of national profile that he deserved. He had other spells where he grabbed the headlines, like during Plymouth's run to the FA Cup semi-final, but really his talent should have been on show at the highest level week in, week out. I can only put it down to not being lucky to get the breaks at the right time as there is no question he was good enough.

Tommy was nearly the complete player. He had decent feet and was a good header of the ball. He was a great passer and had good vision, and made the biggest contribution in our run-in to winning that promotion and Welsh Cup double when playing in a forward midfield role just behind me and big Dave Gwyther. He also had a great awareness of space and that greedy goalscorer's instinct that nearly saw us come to blows one day against our rivals Cardiff City, when he took the ball off my toe with a completely open goal begging – and put it over the bar!

The final thing about Tommy is that he is a bit of a character – well he is a Scouser after all! Tommy knew how to enjoy himself, but no one could ever question his desire to work hard and look after himself. Any of us that had the pleasure of playing with him will not have been surprised to hear of him playing for Argyle against Anderlecht in a friendly just shy of his 50th birthday – and not looking much different to how he did in his playing prime!

So, it is a pleasure to write this foreword and thank him for the hat-trick at Stockport, all of the other 'tricks' he showed me that served me so well during the rest of my career – and to say 'why the hell did you try to steal my goal against Cardiff!'

Cheers Tommy.

Prologue

Monday 12 May 1980

The crowd held its breath as the spinning sphere breached the defence. John Aldridge anticipated the next move and was there to receive the ball. In a second he flicked it up into the air and his cross landed at the feet of Tommy Tynan. Camera flashes danced, chanting ceased, the movement and skill of the two men was poetic and appeared to almost be in slow motion. Psychologists talk of 'the zone', where performance can be enhanced temporarily by intense focus. To achieve this a centre-forward should never take his eye off the ball, yet he also needs to be able to see the opposition and the route to the goal. It takes someone special to develop this instinct and achieve a balance. When Tynan received the cross from Aldridge he knew it was going into the back of the net and the crowd went wild.

It is the ability to consistently put the ball in the net that bonds the crowd with the striker. It is a demanding relationship that can turn nasty when the goals stop coming. The goal mentioned above, which helped Newport County defeat Shrewsbury in the second leg of the Welsh Cup Final, is just one example of Tynan's predatory instinct in the box. It is an instinct that helped him score 33 times during the 1982–83 season, a personal best.

The psychological zone theory cannot stand alone, though, as there also has to be a high level of skill evident in the individual. Refinement comes through repetition and introspection. The dynamic striking partnership that Aldridge and Tynan had was achieved in this way and is still talked about to this day. Although they played together at an early stage in their careers, the amount of goals and assists they created was phenomenal. There are many examples in the archives of such strikers from a truly golden era for Len Ashurst's Newport County as he led the Ironsides to their first silverware, as well as to the quarter-finals of the European Cup-Winners' Cup.

Tommy Tynan was a product of Bill Shankly's Liverpool youth system and he shone at this level. His career took him to many clubs, such as Jack Charlton's Sheffield Wednesday, during a period of great transition. He plied his trade for the Dallas Tornadoes in America, among the likes of George Best and Pelé, where he made a name for himself and built a reputation in the game as a work-hard/play-hard centre-forward with a bright future ahead of him. During the course of his career, Tommy would come under the wing of the great John Charles at Swansea and, of course, he played for other clubs such as Lincoln, Rotherham and at Newport with Aldridge. As a result of his two spells at Plymouth Argyle, he would be voted their greatest-ever player by the fans, who still talk about his 10 goals from nine games during the 1985–86 promotion campaign.

Wednesday 17 December 1997

An angry crowd had gathered outside Home Park. It was the first of several protests against the autocratic chairman of Plymouth Argyle, Dan McCauley. When the results dried up and the crowd were on his back, McCauley had responded by telling the Press he was going to wind the club up. When the story was printed in *The Evening Herald*, McCauley banned them from the ground. The newspaper responded by hiring a crane to lift over the Devonport End for photographs, while the fans also fought back. Chants of 'McCauley out' rang out around the ground; he had gone too far and war was declared. Everything came to a head when McCauley and his wife, Anne, were bombarded with tomatoes during a match. They were also subjected to death threats and told that not even the police could guarantee their safety in the city. It looked like the beginning of the end for Plymouth Argyle.

The protesters may have been calling for McCauley's resignation, but where would the money come from if he left? The man may have been a control freak who liked to know, right down to the last toilet roll, where money had been spent, but he had bailed the club out on several occasions. When players' wages were unpaid he took a quarter of a million pounds out of his own account to cover the cost. A consortium was waiting in the wings with most of the money to buy McCauley out, but they needed a front man. Tommy had only been out of the game for six years and he did not hesitate when asked to mediate and help with fundraising as the money men thrashed out the future of the football club. Around the city stickers and T-shirts were worn in protest with the words 'Plymouth Are Go!' printed on the front. Analysts theorised, talk show hosts speculated and supporters worried during some of the darkest days in the history of the club.

Chapter 1
The Boy Who Got Away

Liverpool was a city that never slept, and as a major English port, it buzzed with activity. World War Two may have taken many of its men, but life there continued, and amid the desolation a rejuvenation was beginning. A post-war boom created jobs as social and economical conditions improved in the city. Rationing ended and the rebuild continued into the 1950s as people began to smile once again. As normal life resumed, the local people began to think about the future. Instead of becoming sailors and soldiers, the men of Liverpool became dockers and shopkeepers, brickies and salesmen. There were even some who used their feet to talk and fashioned an escape from the poverty by becoming professional footballers.

For the working class and his children, watching Liverpool Football Club was the highlight of the week, and to stand in a crowd having a good shout and getting behind the Reds was what Saturday afternoons were all about. Some of the greatest footballers and managers in the history of the game were on display at Anfield during each match, and to imagine being among that elite group was pure escapism. To actually play and learn with such footballing gods was something little boys could only dream of, and standing on the Kop, among a sea of red and white, watching the constant glow of matchstick flames and tobacco smoke from all around, was the nearest most ever came to fulfilling that dream.

To this day Anfield is a place where dreams are constructed by young and old. The noise from the crowd is deafening, persistent chanting bordering on the edge of mass hysteria. To look down at the brilliant green of the floodlit pitch and watch the trickery and skill of those men in red can be inspirational. The dream of playing for 'the 'Pool' is the reason why footballs have been kicked in the streets, parks and housing estates of Liverpool for over 100 years.

In 1950s Liverpool, only the rich had money to spend and luxuries like new cars and TVs were virtually unheard of. Despite the hardship, people were optimistic and a new sense of freedom, which finally emerged in the 1960s, was in the air.

In 1955 the new Queen had been on the throne for just three years and the Tories were beaten in the general election. The 80-year-old Prime Minister Winston Churchill stepped down and Labour's Anthony Eden took up office. Industries in Liverpool such as engineering, shipbuilding, car manufacturing and printing were in decline, a situation that would not change under the new government. This was also the year Martin Luther King started the bus boycotts and the Argentinian president, Juan Peron, was overthrown; the hovercraft, the atomic clock and the polio vaccination were invented and Albert Einstein died. James Dean starred in *East of Eden* and *Rebel Without a Cause* before his tragic death that same year and adverts blazed across the screens of television sets in Britain for the very first time. *The Quatermass Experiment* and *Dixon of Dock Green* were popular TV shows. In the music world Dickie Valentine had pointed his *Finger of Suspicion* all the way to the top in the hit parade by the time Tommy came into the world. A new craze called 'rock 'n' roll' was beginning, but it was not expected to last.

In the world of sport, Chelsea had won their first League title and Newcastle their sixth FA Cup. Rocky Marziano retired as undefeated Heavyweight Boxing Champion and Joe Davis dominated snooker. However, things were not looking good for some of the teams that Tommy would eventually end up playing for. Eric Taylor's Sheffield Wednesday finished bottom of the old First Division, and in Division Two Manchester United legend Jack Rowley became Plymouth Argyle manager just in time to save them from the drop.

Don Welsh's Liverpool finished just above Plymouth in 11th place, their worst season to date, and they were beaten 1–0 by Argyle, followed by a 4–0 defeat at Home Park in successive seasons. Many Reds fans know Welsh as 'the only manager Liverpool ever sacked'. His team were relegated from the First Division in 1954 and immediate promotion was sought to compete with their Merseyside rivals Everton, who were holding their own in the top League. Even the arrival of the legendary Bill Shankly in 1959 could not bring overnight success, and Liverpool remained in Division Two until they were promoted as champions in 1962.

In retrospect it is easy to see how the post-war events in Liverpool have shaped popular culture. In 1963 Bill Shankly's team became League Champions for the first time in 16 years, and the city was at the beginning of a fantastic journey, one that would be written and talked about for many years to come. As the year unfolded it was hard to ignore the beginnings of 'Beatlemania'. Inspired by the music of great rock 'n' roll artists such as Little Richard and Elvis Presley, the Beatles would go on to be one of the biggest acts in the history of popular music.

When flower power hit, an amazing contrast could be seen between old and new. Places like Scotland Road, with its smoky pubs and clubs, were awash with bright colour, and some of the old places were renovated and updated to accommodate a new clientele.

On 17 November 1955 Thomas Edward Tynan was born in Prince Edmond Street, Liverpool, just off Scotland Road. The only son of Thomas and Agnes Tynan, he was the second of three children, his sister Eileen being the eldest, and Elizabeth his younger sister. Football was in the blood of the Tynans. Thomas Snr had turned out for various local sides and his goalkeeping abilities were held in high regard. He had spent most of his working life on Scotland Road working as a fruit porter, like many others who came back from the war. In those days, the place was alive with business, boozing and brawling. There was a pub on every corner and each one was packed with dockers and matlows. Agnes Tynan (née Murphy) was never in good health and spent most of her working life in a biscuit factory nearby. She suffered from fits and died young. Tommy was only 18 years old when she died, but she lived long enough to see her son sign for Liverpool Football Club as an apprentice in 1970. The young footballer was devastated by her death.

Towards the end of the 1950s the Tynans took up residence in Grant Road, Dovecot, which Tommy describes as 'a typical Liverpudlian housing estate'. Everyone was the same on the estates. Nobody had anything and children were lucky if their parents could afford decent food and clothes, let alone a pair of football boots. Tommy was one of the lucky ones as at St Margaret Mary's Catholic School, which he attended from the age of five to 15, a teacher asked some of the locals to donate old football boots. To distribute what had been collected, the teacher told the boys to form an orderly queue, and as he went down the line he tried the boots on all of the boys' feet. Luckily, there was a pair which fitted the youngster and that was how Tommy Tynan got his first pair of boots!

Like a lot of boys, Tommy was always kicking a ball around, emulating his Liverpool heroes. When he was 11 his father took him to Anfield to stand on the Kop for the very first time. From then on he was hooked and did not miss a home match in three seasons. Those magical Anfield nights had such an effect on young Tommy, and when he was not watching Liverpool he was dreaming of being Roger Hunt or Ian St John. Although he would never admit it in public, he would even play as Everton's Alan Ball in the playground cup final.

Life at St Margaret Mary's was harsh and football helped Tommy to escape, and it was not long before his skills were beginning to get him noticed. He spent most of his professional career playing as a forward but started out on the right wing at schoolboy level. You could always find him practising after school as well as running and training, and he loved nothing more than putting the ball in the back of the net. The fruit and vegetables Thomas Snr brought home from work provided a stable diet for all three of the Tynan children, and Tommy had more than enough energy to play for two teams on a Saturday. From an early age his dedication was there for all to see. He looked after himself, kept fit and always went to bed early. His first taste of success came when he played for Liverpool Catholic Schools against Manchester Catholic Schools in the local cup final. The 14-year-old played as a right-sided forward in the match and scored one of the goals as his team went on to win.

As Tommy entered his teenage years he spent a lot of his spare time on 'Scottie' Road helping his dad out with the fruit. He gained a unique insight into the workings and failings of people as well as earning a couple of extra shillings. Unaware of anything out of the ordinary happening around him, he worked and trained hard, learning skills that would stand him in good stead for years to come. As much as he admired the men who ran and organised the daily activities, deep down he knew it was not for him. Little did he know what lay just around the corner.

Looking back at it all today, Tommy never really thought of the characters at Liverpool Football Club as special, to him they were just people. To be respected, of course, but it is only now that they have been elevated to the status of legends. It is easy to forget that such figures were once unknown. It is through sheer determination and hard work that their reputations were built and that Liverpool FC became the global brand it is today. With merchandising and other initiatives, the club is far more than a football team and a world away from 'the old days', when everything seemed so much easier. The pressure on the players today is immense, yet the rewards are beyond the wildest dreams of many people.

A lot of things have been written about Bill Shankly over the years, and it is true that when he arrived at Liverpool in 1959 the club had been in decline for quite some time. Shankly was virtually unknown in management when he took over from Phil Taylor, who had been forced to quit due to ill health. His playing career had started at Carlisle in 1932, where he spent a year, before joining Preston North End. The war interrupted the careers of lots of young footballers, including the 26-year-old Shankly, and many never had the chance to show their skills at the professional level as football was not resumed until 1946. When Bill started playing again he was 33 and he knew his best years were behind him. He was only capped seven times for Scotland, but who knows how many more he would have won if it had not have been for the war?

When Shankly took over at Liverpool he had been in management for a little over 10 years with Carlisle, Grimsby, Workington and Huddersfield. His frustration with others because of their lack of commitment had always been the main reason why he had left his previous appointments. He was originally interviewed for the Liverpool vacancy in 1951, but chairman T.V. Williams did not think he was the right man at the time and he appointed Don Welsh instead. When Shankly finally got the job in 1959 he soon realised that the whole set-up needed an overhaul. The club were still in the Second Division after missing out on promotion yet again, and the stadium and training facilities at Melwood were crumbling. He felt there was too much 'dead wood' in the squad and that too many players were not good enough to wear the red shirt. The original red shirts with white shorts and stockings were soon replaced by the all-red strip of today and Bill thought it made Ron Yeats and the others look harder.

Shankly's 'pass and move' style of football took in the basic elements of the game and was like the football he had seen played as a child in Scotland by the Glenbuck Miners. For the system to work a solid team performance was required. Individual flair was always sought, but the basic premise, which held team spirit intact, was that the players had to play quick football, even if an individual was having a bad day. Tommy remembers:

'It is quite surprising how much of the Liverpool way rubbed off on me really. Shankly's style of pass, move and wait for an opening, or create one yourself, didn't always produce the prettiest football but it got results, and it was certainly indoctrinated in me.'

To help his team to bond, Shankly encouraged them to spend more time together eating and socialising, which was a massive gamble because if the team were to build an understanding and a tolerance of one another, all the time they spent together had to be a pleasure rather than a chore. The training methods Shankly used were also revolutionary, for example by encouraging a warm-down after activity, players picked up fewer injuries. These now much-copied methods were very quickly instilled in the team and allowed Shankly to cut down the number of players he needed to draft into the side from the reserve teams. It is interesting to note that during the Championship-winning season of 1965–66, only 14 players were used all season and two of those only played in a handful of games. It was a trend that would continue, and many young players, including Tommy, missed out.

By the mid-1970s the level of quality coming through the youth ranks at Liverpool was so high that two teams of equal ability could have been fielded. Shankly's backroom team have been referred to on many occasions as 'The Boot Room' and all of them had an impact on Tommy as he learned his trade. During the rebuild Shankly insisted the development of youth was made a priority, as it was vital to the future. Tom Saunders came to the club in 1968. He had been recommended by Tony Waiters and his roll was to assist Bob Paisley and his coaches. Shankly's first great team were beginning to get old and now was the time for Bill to set aside personal loyalty and swing the axe. Thus began the second rebuild, and Saunders was just the man to help. He was a local man and a headmaster, who spent all his spare time coaching Liverpool and England schoolboys. He had enjoyed a modest playing career with teams such as Fleetwood and Marine but really found his niche under Shankly coaching the youngsters. His words, as well as those of Reuben Bennett, provided a focal point for the youngsters. To stand on that Melwood turf in the middle of December in nothing more than boots, shorts and a bib took a lot of dedication. With the wind and rain pelting down, the young players needed the inner warmth of blind determination as well as the will to succeed. The inspiring commands of Saunders from the touchline, hidden beneath a big coat, mixed with Bennett, the persistent driving voice, had the desired effect. Their insistent tones inspired players to moments of sheer brilliance and flair. Bennett had come to Liverpool in 1958 and was brought in by former manager Phil Taylor. He had worked with Bill Shankly's brother, Bob, at Dundee after the war and had played as a goalkeeper for Hull City, Dundee United and Queen of the South before the conflict began.

Malcolm Allison described Tom Saunders as 'the only real youth development officer' and the advice he gave the young players really could inspire. He sat Tommy and the rest of the youth team down to tell them about the riches of football in the early 1970s. Among the group of 17 or so apprentices Saunders assembled that day were future Liverpool legends Phil Thompson, Alan Kennedy, David Fairclough and Jimmy Case. He told them that if they put football first they could have anything they wanted, and money, cars and women were a good enough reason for Tommy to 'get his head down'.

He knew some of them would not make it in professional football and he told them straight. He also told them they would remember the day and his words for the rest of their lives and time has proved him right.

In 1970 the quality of youths coming through the ranks had to improve, and Shankly and his generals knew something had to be done to sort out the situation.

Chapter 2
Anfield Education

By 1970 the Liverpool team was being rebuilt and young blood was needed. In the local newspaper, *The Liverpool Echo*, a fantastic competition was launched. It was the biggest competition ever and every boy's dream. The parks and pitches of the city were alive with wannabes kicking balls as the search for a star began. Three decades before reality television programmes became popular, the newspaper, along with the club, was challenging young players to test themselves and see if they could win. The prize was an apprenticeship at Bill Shankly's famous Liverpool Football Club and the chance to become the original 'Football Idol'. Tommy remembers:

'It all came about because there wasn't much happening in the reserves. A lot of the 1960s team were over the hill and I guess Bill came up with the 'Search for a Star' thing to give local lads a chance.'

There were 10,000 entrants and coupons had to be cut out and posted. Tommy would wait until his dad had eaten his evening meal and nodded off in his armchair with the newspaper crumpled between his knees before he would make ready with a pair of scissors out of his mother's drawer in the kitchen. The story was the same all across Liverpool, with many bemused parents discovering their newspapers in ruins. On the final night of trials, one cold evening in 1970, the 10,000 entrants had been whittled down to just 22. Shankly and his men stood on the sideline of the

A team pitch at Melwood and watched the activities before them, occasionally passing comment or jotting something down. The whole event consisted of four five-a-side matches and the first match started at 6pm. As the young Tommy made his way out onto the pitch, he shivered beneath the floodlights, it was a chilly night but the immensity of the occasion was also having an effect. After the final trial nothing was said, but Tommy's team had won 5–3 and he had scored all five goals. Shankly and the rest of the coaches thanked the boys and exchanged a few words and handshakes with some of the watching dads before heading for their cars. When Tommy arrived home that night the adrenaline was still pumping around his body, he knew he had done well but he lay in bed replaying the events in his head, not really comprehending what this day would mean to the rest of his life.

'The next day there was a knock at the door – it was John Bennison, Tom Saunders's assistant. My dad led Bennison into the house and he asked for permission to take me to Anfield to train. I was 15 years old and delighted and we went off to Anfield immediately. Mum and Dad were as proud as peacocks – after the hours we had spent on the Kop, now I was going to Anfield to meet Bill Shankly. Dad had seen Hunt and St John setting Anfield alight, and had nicknamed St John 'spring-heels' because of the magnificent goals he scored with his head, so he was absolutely made up that his boy would be playing on the same Anfield turf as those great men.'

Within the club's structure were four sides: the first team, the reserves and the A and B teams, much as it is today, and Tommy was invited to Melwood to train with the A and B teams, while the coaches assessed his ability. To begin with he was asked to drop back or run channels on the right wing, but he was never happy there. He was not just a forward-thinking player, but an instinctive goalscorer, as he went on to prove throughout his career. At each level he had the opportunity to play at, he rewarded the manager with goals.

Soon, Tommy was excelling as a centre-forward, becoming leading goalscorer for the reserves as well as the A and B teams, and an injury to Kevin Keegan led him to within touching distance of the first team. However, on that day another youngster, Jimmy Case, got the nod ahead of Tommy. In 1970 it was not possible for a 15-year-old to sign as an apprentice for a professional football club, so Tommy had to wait until his 16th birthday in November. The Press were assembled with their cameras to record the moment, as were Shankly and other members of his staff. It was the end of the swinging 60s but the beginning of a football career for Tommy Tynan.

Dominating the news in 1970 were stories about the continuing US nuclear tests in the Nevada desert and Charles De Gaulle's death. In Bangladesh 3.5 million people were killed by a 240kph cyclone, while the Russians put a vehicle on the moon. A dagger-wielding painter dressed as a priest wounded Pope Paul VI in the Philippines and the first live cell was artificially synthesised.

In Liverpool at the end of the year Paul McCartney started proceedings to sue his band-mates, which ultimately led to the breakup of the Beatles. However, in footballing terms the run-up to Christmas 1970 saw the Liverpool first team play nine games. In November they were held to a 0–0 draw at home to Coventry, 10 days after drawing 1–1 with Dynamo Bucharest at home in the Fairs Cup. They went through 4–1 on aggregate, with Phil Boersma scoring the only goal that night, a player who later proved to be a great help to Tommy as he found his way around the club, giving him the advice and energy he needed to keep his head held high among all of the superstars around him. The month ended with a 2–0 defeat to Arsenal down at Highbury. The Christmas period was another mixed period for the first team as they picked up a win and three draws in the League. They did well in the Fairs Cup, however, knocking Scottish side Hibernian out in the third round, but their overall form that season was not good enough to win the League. In the FA Cup that season Liverpool met Arsenal again at Wembley but they were beaten again that day in front of 100,000 fans as Arsenal did the first League and FA Cup double since Tottenham Hotspur a decade earlier.

Tommy was training and playing with the A and B teams and beginning to settle at the club. By the summer of 1971 the A team had lost only four out of 46 games, an impressive season. The statistics were not quite so favourable for the B team, who only managed to win seven out of the 28 games they played that year. They were beaten 7–0 on 3 October by Tranmere Reserves, who turned them over again 8–1 at Prenton Park. The problem was the quality of some of the youth players coming up through the ranks, and it was apparent that there were many players who were just not up to the job.

The country is full of ex-players and non-League 30-somethings who, at an early stage in their careers, had the potential to unlock defences, slam the ball into the back of the net or make the most magnificent save at the highest level in the game. For one reason or another that potential has failed to be reached and the talent wasted. Bill Shankly believed players reached the peak of their game at around 28 years old and many years of development already needed to have occurred. Today, managers talk about protecting younger players as the late teen years are a crucial time for development and 100 per cent dedication is a minimum requirement to make it as a professional. At Liverpool Shankly applied a kind of quiet discipline to his team and Tommy soon learned the Liverpool way. There was no place for womanising, drinking and partying in the Shankly doctrine. On most occasions the boss knew more about a player's general attitude than they did themselves. A legion of coaches, scouts and spies would be deployed around the towns and grounds before anybody put pen to paper.

Shankly instilled a sense of order to a club that had been in decline for a number of years. Young players coming in had to hit the ground running, and Tommy soon experienced his first taste of the discipline and effort required. As long as you gave it your best Shankly would build you up, instilling confidence in the individual and belittling the opposition. It was psychological warfare. It is very difficult to discover just how much of his own propaganda he really believed. Before a match he would routinely run opposing players down and praise them for what they were really worth only after the full-time whistle. On one occasion he told Kevin Keegan that opposition defender Bobby Moore was getting old and looked like he had been out drinking all night. His words had the desired effect and Keegan had an outstanding game – on the pitch he had felt no fear for the World Cup-winning captain because of Shankly's comments. After the match Shankly said to Keegan, 'Jesus Christ, did you see that Bobby Moore? He's some player…'

Another amusing example occurred when Shankly signed Emlyn Hughes from Blackpool. He had insisted on picking up the player and driving him back down to Liverpool, but on the way back they were pulled over by the police. Shankly wound down his window and told the policeman that he was looking at the next England captain, it was typical Bill. When we look back at such events we must remember the myths that have grown up around Bill Shankly. Readily we accept that such comments were prophecies or insight. Indeed, Shankly made a lot of statements, some of which he only half believed. He did not need to shout the odds or go to the Press, a player knew by his silence and insistent pacing that the boss was not amused. There were, of course, occasions when cups and saucers flew, but this was not commonplace.

Shankly's psychological manipulation did not always work though. Another famous outburst came during the 1971–72 season, when before an important Cup-Winners' Cup match he called the great Bayern Munich side more of a Christmas club than a football club. Liverpool lost on the night and Bayern marched on to win three European Cups. Perhaps Shankly did not take himself seriously at times, as such tactics were only designed to get the players into the right state of mind for the match ahead and it usually worked.

Tommy remembers the Scot as having a kind of aura around him, and when he entered the room people receded into the background. Most days Shankly would gather his staff in the legendary boot room, where they would sit on upturned crates and discuss the team while he brewed tea. The room, as its name suggests, was 12ft square and full of boots, balls and bibs and has been elevated to mythical status over the years. Tommy remembers:

> *'Access to the boot room was restricted, if you were a player you came to get your boots and that was it. If a bollocking was coming your way it usually happened in the office.'*

The boot room was finally pulled down during the Graeme Souness era as he disposed of many things Shankly had put in place, much to his detriment.

Drawing a comparison between Shankly and modern-day managers is difficult because the game today is very different. Bill was old school and he liked things done his way with minimal interference from the board, which was one of the conditions when he became manager in 1959. Back in the 1960s, it was not as easy to travel around Europe as it is today. Although Liverpool were able to charter planes for European games later on, it is interesting to ponder what Shankly would have made of modern technology and modern managers.

What would he have made of the increasing non-contact nature of the game and the multi-million pound teams whose players get flown everywhere, drive posh cars and earn enough money to feed a small country? Shankly believed the fans were the important people and his ways, and others such as Matt Busby and Brian Clough, are gone forever. On his retirement Shankly had a few quid, but he was not rich, but when a top-class player or manager retires from the game today they are set for life.

Tommy remembers Bill as a very competitive person – it was in his nature and he did not like to lose. During a five-a-side staff versus apprentices match Tommy took his turn between the sticks and he remembers:

> *'I remember that the staff line up for the five-a-side match was Bill Shankly, John Bennison, Tom Saunders, Roy Evans and Reuben Bennett, who couldn't run and had to have the ball played to his feet outside of the D. Shankly was awarded a penalty that I managed to save. All of a sudden he is demanding that the shot be retaken shouting, "You must have moved son!" I was only a kid and you can't argue with the gaffer, and he slotted the ball into the back of the net on the second attempt. Everybody knew the staff always won the five-a-side games and Bill would simply play until they were ahead and then blow the full-time whistle, that's how crafty he was!'*

Despite the fun and games, the five-a-side matches helped Liverpool to perfect their style and soon other managers were doing the same. The football was not always pretty, and Shankly had his critics, but it produced results. Players were encouraged to keep the ball and create space. The key was in possession and careful build-up. The pressure would usually get to the opposition and then an opening would arise. Players like Peter Cormack, with his silky passing, really benefitted from those five-a-side games. The man-management players enjoy today was not commonplace back then, Shankly and Bob Paisley, who was a trained physiotherapist, coached their teams in a very different way. With the knowledge and technology available today, managers and coaches are able to scrutinise and control things like nutrition and training in ways Shankly and his staff could not. At all professional clubs nowadays you will find specialist coaches for all positions, but when Tommy was learning his trade you just had to get on with it:

'It was so different then, you know, going out for a few pints wasn't frowned upon as much as it is today and I don't think the media was so intense just as long as you didn't go daft. And the eating, it's a lot more scientific today but we were expected to look after ourselves.'

The two training pitches at Melwood were excellent and provided fantastic surfaces for the youngster to learn on. No matter what the weather was like or which team were playing, Bill Shankly would always be there in the background, barely visible. He spent many hours simply watching, not interfering with the work of his coaches but quietly reckoning things up in his mind. He always seemed to know when an individual had had enough or was carrying an injury. Famous for ignoring players if they were injured in a match, he could be stood silently watching from the sideline for an hour or more before passing comment to a player or to one of his staff. He was good at assessing a player's ability and the effect they were having on the balance of the team, and he would suggest that a player could be more effective by playing at such-and-such a position or by passing the ball to so-and-so. Tommy was encouraged to get in between the centre-halves and run off them while bearing in mind his positioning. He always knew where the goal was and it was just a matter of a chance arising. Scoring goals is not something that can be learned from a textbook, goalscorers are, as Tommy says, 'born and not made'.

Apart from the five-a-side matches, a lot of the training consisted of positioning work, such as where to start and finish a run for corners, crosses and set pieces. This was practised on the training ground and all of the players were conditioned to the Liverpool way, which was to just get out there and play football. As well as training, the apprentices were also given other jobs and when Tommy was not playing, his other duties included sweeping the stands, cleaning the changing rooms and toilets and anything else that needed to be done. It was also his job to clean the boots of England goalkeeper Ray Clemence, whom Tommy describes as 'a lovely bloke who still owes him £2'.

It wouldn't be long before Tommy was playing regularly for the reserves and the youth teams throughout his early apprentice days, alongside players like Jimmy Case, Sammy Lee and Phil Thompson, who was in his final year in the youth team. Tom Saunders soon recognised Tommy was better suited as a striker and he played up front regularly. One of his first big matches for Liverpool was the 1972 FA Youth Cup Final, but Liverpool lost 3–2 to Aston Villa. However, the youngster raised a few eyebrows that day with his attacking play and he spent the summer training hard to become as fit as he could. When he returned to Anfield for pre-season training he was looking for a chance to stake a claim in the first team.

Chapter 3
Hitting the
Ground Running

Joining Liverpool FC required dedication and players had to get fit and work hard to become a regular player, but lots of lads were envious. It made the blond-haired footballer quite a catch for the local girls! All-night parties and binge-drinking were just as popular among teenagers back then. There have been so many young footballers who have become caught up in the lifestyle and over-consumed, but Tommy was lucky, he knew he could never live like that if he was going to make a career out of professional football. He never touched cigarettes and this certainly helped him in terms of fitness. Such self-discipline, coupled with the fact he always had a ball at his feet and little time for anything else, steered him away from some of the pitfalls and temptations teenagers commonly experience. He had seen his mother die from cancer and as he progressed throughout his early career the memory of what she went through was never far away from his thoughts. Terminal cancer, in its many forms, is a terrible disease, not just for the sufferer but also for the family and carers. Tommy lost both of his parents to cancer and is the reason why he has never smoked.

When writing Tommy's life story it is important to recreate as true a reflection of the events and times as possible. It is therefore necessary to talk about the highs and lows alongside all the fantastic moments which occurred throughout his career. Tommy has mentioned times when he has broken the rules and gone out on the town with a few other players before a big game, but he has never been involved in, or been offered, any kind of illegal substance or been asked to fix a game. He will admit to wearing a plastic bag under his kit during training to sweat alcohol out of his system after a night on the tiles but he has never contemplated enhancing his performance artificially.

Maybe Tommy managed to stay on the straight and narrow because for him it was never about the money or the recognition. From an early age he was always running around kicking some kind of ball about so the game was in his blood. Even though playing for Liverpool was a bit different to a kick-about in the street, the same passion had to be there.

The 1971–72 season had ended with Brian Clough's Derby County finishing as League Champions for the first time in their history. Liverpool finished third behind Leeds United, who also won the FA Cup, beating Arsenal 1–0 at Wembley. It was also the season that Stoke City beat Chelsea 2–1 in the League Cup Final and Ajax won the second of three consecutive European Cups. While the summer was in full swing, West Germany won the European Championships for the first time, beating England along the way. Back in Liverpool, Kings Waterfront, part of the South Liverpool docking system, was being used for the very last time. Formerly known as Kings Dock, the closure was a significant moment in the scaling down of Liverpool's industries. Apart from livelihoods being threatened, the other thing on the minds of many locals was the fact that it had been six years since Shankly and his team had won their last major honour when they finished as the League champions. Despite finishing as runners-up in the 1971 FA Cup Final, the fans were beginning to get restless and felt in need of some more silverware. While cinemas played *The Godfather* and *Fist of Fury*, and Donny and Jimmy Osmond dominated the music charts, Tommy was learning the difference between the standards of a professional footballer compared with an amateur player. Behind the scenes Shankly and his generals were plotting the season ahead like it was a military campaign. Little did they know that the League trophy would be arriving back in Liverpool in less than 12 months.

The 1972–73 season started with two wins and a draw for the Liverpool first team. They played their first League match on 12 August and comfortably beat Manchester City 3–0 at Anfield in front of over 50,000 fans. On the same day, Tommy found himself playing for the reserves as they went down by a goal to nil at Everton. Three days later the first team and the reserves were in action once more. The first team faced Manchester United at home and won 2–0, with goals coming from John Toshack and Steve Heighway. It was the start of a very poor season for United who finished it in 18th position, only two places above the drop zone. The reserves were away again that day, this time against Blackpool, and they lost 2–0. The third match of the season was on 19 August and the first team beat Crystal Palace 1–0 while the reserves beat Derby County 3–2, with goals coming from Cormack, Waddington and Kewley, who was, incidentally, destined to cross the Atlantic with Tommy in 1976 as they spent the summer playing in America.

On 7 October 1972 the League match at Anfield between Liverpool and the old enemy Everton finished one-a-piece. Everton finished in 17th position that season, only one place above Manchester United. A week later, and just a month before his 17th birthday, Tommy scored his first goal for Liverpool reserves in a 4–1 win against Huddersfield Town. Future Liverpool legend Phil Thompson was also among the goalscorers that day, as were Kewley and McLaughlin. Tommy was soon scoring lots of goals for both the A and B teams.

His five goals from seven appearances were just the beginning of a prolific goalscoring spree for the reserves, which finished with a magnificent hat-trick against Stoke City reserves in his last match in a red shirt on 7 September 1976.

After his apprenticeship Tommy signed professional forms for Liverpool on 27 November 1972, when he was 17 years old. The stars of the previous few years had gone and the youngster was learning his trade among a group of new players, many of whom went on to become the nucleus of one of the greatest footballing sides in the history of the game. To be among people like Ray Clemence, Tommy Smith and Emlyn Hughes was an education in itself. By the end of the decade Liverpool had won many trophies both home and abroad, so there could surely be no better football education at the time than an Anfield education.

By March the first team were on their way to becoming League Champions. They went on to finish the season with 60 points, with Arsenal in second place and Leeds third.

The team did not have any luck in the domestic Cups, which may have helped them to focus their attention on the UEFA Cup. After taking some notable scalps in the early rounds, Liverpool lined up against holders Tottenham in the semi-final. On 10 April 1973 Liverpool beat Spurs 1–0 at Anfield, before losing 2–1 at White Hart Lane. With an aggregate score of two-a-piece, Liverpool went through on away goals. This set them up for a showdown in the Final and on 10 May they faced Borussia Mönchengladbach at Anfield in the first leg. This was the second attempt at staging the match as the rain had fallen torrentially the previous day and the match had to be abandoned after half an hour as the pitch turned into a lake. In that half an hour Shankly had seen enough of the Germans to realise that their weakness was in the air. To rectify this he brought John Toshack back into the team for the rescheduled match. It was an inspired move and a night that will always be remembered by those who were there. Kevin Keegan scored two goals, both of which were set up by Toshack, and Larry Lloyd put the ball into the back of the net in the 62nd minute for the third. The noise was deafening and Liverpool won, with Ray Clemence saving a crucial penalty.

They took a comfortable 3–0 lead to the Bokelbergstadion for the second leg. After a nervy first half they were two-down with both goals coming from Heynckes. As they left the pitch at half-time they could feel the match slipping away from them. Luckily the Germans had all but burned themselves out, and as the second half progressed Liverpool began to get back into the match. Borussia had run out of steam and by the last third Liverpool looked as dangerous as they had in the first leg. The match ended with a famous 3–2 victory, and Shankly and his team had their first European trophy in the bag.

In the music world 1973 also saw David Bowie become the biggest seller since the Beatles, and Slade notched up three number-one singles. In the cinema films such as *The Exorcist* and *Live and Let Die* were released to worldwide acclaim, while the chopper became Britain's best selling push-bike (they even produced a bike to celebrate daring motorcycle stuntman Evel Knievel).

This was also the year Tommy had his one and only brush with the England Youth squad. Tom Saunders juggled his duties at Liverpool with his position as England's Youth manager. Saunders was in a unique position because of his involvement with both and was able to view young players and make recommendations to Shankly and Paisley. There was a lot of talent in the England Youth team at the time, as there was in Scotland, which Saunders also kept an eye on. Soon the exodus of Scottish players to Liverpool would be in full swing with young Scottish players such as Kenny Dalglish, Graeme Souness and Alan Hansen joining the Reds.

In 1973 Tommy's girlfriend Rita became pregnant. She had a baby girl and the young couple were married, but they were both 18 years old and far too young for marriage.

'We were living in my dad's back room and we had no money. It was a bit of a strain for everyone. Rita decided it would be best if she went with the baby to her mother's. Soon after I moved club. Things got awkward then and we lost touch. We were just too young. I made sure I continued to pay maintenance but she settled down, it was all pretty horrible. I suppose I deal with it by telling myself I'm only a father in the biological sense, I wasn't there to bring her up.'

Chapter 4
Goals, Goals, Goals!

Tommy's most prolific period at Liverpool had been for the A team when he scored an amazing 13 goals from five games, but still without so much as a sniff at the first team. That was how good the squad was. Despite spending time on loan with Swansea City and the Dallas Tornadoes, Tommy still scored 48 goals in 86 games for the reserves, an average of well over a goal every other game. It is a situation which he recalls with a smile and not a hint of 'what if?'.

Liverpool opened their 1973–74 campaign with a 1–0 win at home to Stoke City on 25 August. Tommy travelled with the reserves to Newcastle, where they also won by the same score, with the goal coming from McLaughlin. Tommy was feeling fitter than he had done in previous seasons and the extra training throughout the summer had given him a little bit of an edge when he reported back for pre-season training. The reserves followed the Newcastle game with another win at Bolton Wanderers; it was to be another good season as they won the Central League. Tommy's first goals of the 1973–74 season came on 13 October at home as he grabbed two for the reserves, sweeping Nottingham Forest aside in a 4–0 victory. On the same day the first team were beaten by Southampton at The Dell and they were eventually beaten to the League title by Leeds United.

Three days before Christmas Tommy scored two for the reserves against Manchester United. They were the only goals of the match and marked another excellent display. He was now 19 years old and really beginning to find his feet. His performances and goals had started people talking. On 12 January he hit another in a 3–1 win, with Case and Boersma getting the others. His goal against Everton a week later was particularly sweet and the match finished with a 2–0 victory for the Reds. It had taken Tommy a while to get into the swing of things that season, and when he scored his first goals against Nottingham Forest the reserves had already played 12 League games. Alan Waddle had already netted on six occasions for the reserves before the game, but by mid-January Tommy had overtaken him. He grabbed the season by scoring the winner against Stoke City in a 3–2 win and the reserves won the Central League once again.

In the Liverpool Senior Cup they were beaten 3–2 by Tranmere, with Tommy scoring Liverpool's second four minutes from time.

In 1974 Bill Shankly left due to ill health and, even though the team failed to win he title, he was delighted to sign off by winning his second FA Cup. It had not been an easy road to the Final, and two replays were required along the way. The first was against Doncaster Rovers, a team which Tommy would turn out for towards the end of his career. Doncaster finished third from bottom in the Fourth Division in 1974 but still managed a one-all draw at Anfield in the third round. The replay attracted 22,000 people to Belle Vue, but Doncaster's luck ran out that day and they were beaten 2–0. The second replay occurred in the semi-final when Liverpool drew with Leicester City at Old Trafford before finally beating them at Villa Park. The Reds beat Newcastle 3–0 in the Final with Keegan grabbing a brace and Heighway scoring the third.

Despite finishing as top scorer in the reserves once again, there was still no call-up for Tommy to the first team. He had begun to wonder just what he had to do to impress Bill Shankly, who had nurtured his talent and seen him become a highly competent goalscorer for the second string, but before he got the chance to ask Bill had retired. Bill sadly died in the early hours of Tuesday 29 September 1981 at Broadgreen Hospital after suffering a massive heart attack when he was only 68 years old. However, his achievements for Liverpool Football Club remain his enduring legacy.

Bob Paisley took over as manager after Bill Shankly retired and his approach to management was different to his predecessor's. Despite all the good work he had done in assisting Shankly, he was still unproven as a manager in his own right so there was a little apprehension about the future from the fans and players. Paisley's previous role meant he was his natural successor and it was not long before he had settled into his new job. Tommy has this to say about the managerial changeover:

'Paisley knew Bill Shankly's system better than anyone so in that sense he was his natural successor. In the beginning I don't think he wanted it though. Bill had been the focal point and it must have been daunting. The two men were very different – they had different elements of genius. Shankly was very intense and imposing.'

The Reds opened their League campaign on 17 August 1974 with a 2–1 win at Kenilworth Road against Luton Town, with Smith and Heighway grabbing the goals. The reserves opened on the same day with a one-all home draw against Bolton Wanderers, and Tommy scored the goal. It was the beginning of another prolific season for the youngster, who had bagged six by Christmas.

The start of the year saw the government stepping in to bail out Burmah Oil, Britain's second largest oil company and in the music world, Ralph McTell topped the charts with his hit *Streets of London*. Back in the reserves, Tommy had to wait until the 29th of the month for his eighth goal of the season, which came in a 2–1 win at home to Newcastle. A day after the election of Margaret Thatcher as Conservative party leader on the 11 February, Liverpool's first team were thrashed 4–1 at Newcastle, but six weeks later they turned the tables on their old foes, thrashing them 4–0 at Anfield. On 15 March Tommy hit two more against Burnley in a 5–1 win at their place, a day before Malcolm Macdonald became the first England player to score five in a match as they thrashed minnows Cyprus 5–0 at Wembley. Tommy grabbed another two on 22 March and the 19-year-old's goals steered the team to the Central League title once again.

There were four more goals from him in April, one against Everton, two against Wolves and the last against Coventry City on the 22nd. In the FA Cup Final West Ham beat Fulham 2–0, with West Ham and England legend Bobby Moore missing out on the silverware with new team Fulham. Luton, Chelsea and Carlisle were relegated from the old First Division and Manchester United were promoted as Champions of Division Two, while Tommy's future employers, Sheffield Wednesday, finished bottom.

During the close season of 1975 *Jaws*-mania was gripping cinemas, alongside *Monty Python's Holy Grail* and Stanley Kubrick's *One Flew Over the Cuckoo's Nest*. On 21 June the West Indies won the first cricket World Cup at Lords with Captain Clive Lloyd scoring an excellent 102. For the start of the new season, Bob Paisley was unveiling new signing Joey Jones to play alongside Terry McDermott and Phil Neal, who had arrived at the club at the end of 1974.

After a short break Tommy was back in training gearing up for pre-season matches for what would be his final full season at Anfield. The 1975–76 season was one of goals and a number of changes for Tommy Tynan.

Chapter 5
League Debut

Bob Paisley was sitting in his office one day in the summer of 1975 when the phone rang. Upon answering it, he found it was his friend Harry Griffith on the other end. Harry was the manager of Fourth Division Swansea City and he was keen to take Tommy on loan.

Nicknamed *The Rocket*, most people involved in local football in and around Swansea during the 1970s had a tale to tell about Harry Griffith. He was a larger-than-life character who met with a tragic end. Capped just once for Wales, he was a powerful left-back who liked to get forward, very much like many left-backs in the game today. His reign as Swansea City manager is sometimes overshadowed by his successor John Toshack, who became player-manager in March 1978, but Griffith will always be remembered by the most ardent of fans for his exciting style of football, a style Swans fans had not seen for many years. Griffith's ways and methods are now resigned to the past, and he loved Swansea City Football Club with a passion rarely seen in the game today. He did not mind getting his hands dirty and carried out most of the jobs at the club, from team manager to sweeping the changing rooms, during his time there. When Toshack took over he did not see Harry as a threat, more as part of the furniture, but he realised that he knew the club better than anyone else. He became Toshack's number two and together they built a promotion-winning team. Griffith later died tragically at The Vetch in the medicine room after he suffered a massive heart attack, and it was a shock to everyone involved with the club.

Tommy was still no nearer to making his first-team debut, and Bob

Paisley was only too aware of this. In an era when multiple substitutes were not allowed, there was little room for making changes to the first team even though Tommy had a great scoring record for the reserves, so, barring a major bout of flu or a natural disaster, Tommy was unlikely to make a start in the first team; there were just too many players ahead of him at Anfield. Paisley felt a loan move would be a good opportunity for Tommy as it would give him the chance to play first-team football. It would also provide an opportunity to make a few headlines, which could of course stir interest from other clubs.

When Tommy arrived in Swansea for a month's loan in 1975, he discovered the facilities at the Vetch Field were somewhat dilapidated. He lodged in a bed and breakfast on the seafront owned by former Swans player Mel Nurse, and he remembers the time with fondness. He admits that he would have liked to stay at Swansea for a bit longer but the club did not have sufficient funds. He let Griffith know from the start of the loan that he was not interested in a permanent move because he still felt he had a chance of breaking into the first team on his return to Anfield. He knew that the football world was rarely static and that things were changing all of the time, so he felt that all he needed was a lucky break and a chance in the Liverpool first team would arise.

Tommy made his League debut for Swansea at Belle Vue against Doncaster Rovers on 18 October 1975, and, despite being beaten 2–1, he scored his first goal on his debut. After making six appearances for the Swans and scoring two goals, he planned his return to Anfield, unaware that the loan move to Swansea would signal the end of his time at Liverpool and that he would have to move away from his boyhood team to continue his professional career. Tommy says

'It just didn't seem like it was a move in the right direction, but now I think to myself, maybe I should have stayed in with Harry Griffith and John Charles. It's all well and good in hindsight but I had no reason to believe it wouldn't work out at Liverpool then.'

From the day Tommy first stepped onto that Anfield turf he had listened to and learned everything his teachers had told him, and he felt he had done everything that had been asked of him. He recalls his four years at Liverpool with incredible fondness, but he always knew that there were some very talented people who would establish world-class reputations, which would make it tough to get a first-team place. There really is no way anyone who was not involved can imagine what it was like to be part of the Liverpool set-up during the reign of Shankly and Paisley. Those days are now the stuff of legend.

Harry Griffith was disappointed that he was not able to extend Tommy's loan period, but there was nothing he could do about it – there was just no money at that level of the game back then. There were not many people then who thought about playing or managing as a means of gaining vast wealth. The notion of a golden handshake was unheard of; a severance payment might keep a sacked manager or a released player from the dole queue for a little while, but nothing more. It must have made being bottom of the League with a couple of thousand fans on your case even more nerve-wracking when you had to put food on the table and coins in the electric, not that Harry was ever involved in a relegation scuffle during his time as manager. In his first season, 1975–76, the season when Tommy came on loan, the Swans finished 11th in the Fourth Division, and the following season they just missed out on promotion, amassing a massive 82 goals and finishing fifth with 58 points.

The Vetch Field would never have won any awards for beauty and narrowly avoided being a gasworks before it was built. The facilities were worlds away from Melwood and Anfield, and until the club moved out in the early part of the 21st century players trained on the beaches around Swansea in the icy cold with the ocean snapping at their heels. People walking dogs or coming home from parties or nightshifts would stop for a cigarette and watch the players as they were put through their paces, and if they were lucky they caught a glimpse of Swansea's youth-team coach John Charles, who is regarded by many as the greatest Welsh footballer of all time and is remembered alongside the likes of Best, Pelé and Maradona. He was born in Cwmbwrla in Swansea on 27 December 1931 but he never played for his home team. Instead, he joined Leeds United in January 1949, earning the princely sum of £10 a week. He later became a goalscoring legend at Juventus in Italy. Charles also set a record for Wales by becoming the youngest player to wear a red shirt at the tender age of 18 years and 71 days. This record stood until 1992, when Manchester United's Ryan Giggs finally beat it. Tommy describes him as an absolute gentleman who loved his country and his football.

During his month with Swansea City, Tommy's performances caught the eye of not only the manager but also his coaches. Indeed, his performances led to Charles making Tommy what was possibly the biggest offer of his life at that point, and the one regret he has about his playing days occurred on that day – he said 'no' to the great man, who had obviously seen something special. Charles wanted him to go to Italy at the end of the season to play in a tournament – he took a young team out there every summer – and it may have sent Tommy's career soaring off in a completely different direction. Tommy now firmly believes that playing in Italy could have opened doors for him and given him a much bigger stage on which to show what he could do. Hindsight, however, is a marvellous thing, but it is too late when all those unstructured whims and mystical half-hidden thoughts suddenly become as clear as day. What we must remember here is that Tommy still believed he would make the first team when he re-joined Liverpool from Swansea and he was not looking to impress on far-off shores. In his mind he was with the Swans for a bit of first-team experience, and although he enjoyed his time with the club, playing first-team football was the sole purpose of the move.

If he had known then that his days were numbered at Anfield, he would have gone to Italy. The problem was that he was enjoying himself at Liverpool and did not see any reason to go abroad, despite Charles's reputation. The Italians loved John Charles like he was one of their own; he knew the big players in Italian football and was well respected. Tommy recalls that years after Charles had finished playing he flew into Italy where he was greeted by a crowd holding up banners and shouting 'Charlo, Charlo!'

In history, 1975 was the year that *Viking I* was launched by NASA, Rembrandt's painting, *Nightwatch*, was slashed 12 times in an Amsterdam gallery and US President Gerard Ford survived two assassination attempts. It was also the year Bill Gates first used the term 'Micro-Soft' in a letter to Paul Allen, but for Tommy it was the year he finally made his League debut, finished top scorer for the reserves and turned down John Charles's offer.

Back in Liverpool, the first team started the 1975–76 season poorly. Although they finished up as League Champions, they had started on 16 August with a 2–0 defeat away to Queen's Park Rangers. Three days later, they could only manage a two-all draw at home to West Ham, with goals coming from Callaghan and Toshack. When Tommy returned from his loan spell, he scored his first two goals for the reserves on 6 December in a 5–3 win at Blackburn. He followed this with the only two goals at home to Burnley on the 13th and did not score again until 15 January 1976, when they lost 3–2 at home to Huddersfield. His last goal of the season came on 19 March when the reserves beat Sheffield Wednesday 2–0 at their place.

Chapter 6
Summer of '76

The summer of 1976 will always be remembered for the heatwave in England. As temperatures soared, standpipes were fitted and people had to queue in the streets for water. There was not much else to do but head for the beach. Bob Paisley had now been in charge of Liverpool for two years and the team were on the way to becoming the best side in the world, so Tommy knew his chance of staking a claim in the first team had vanished. Shankly's young signings were beginning to blossom and Paisley had added players like Phil Neal, Terry McDermott and Joey Jones to the mix. Sammy Lee had come up through the ranks and soon Alan Hansen, Kenny Dalglish and Graeme Souness would be pulling on a red shirt too. Tommy was fast approaching his 21st birthday and was desperate to play first-team football. However, despite some decent performances and goals scored he was no nearer to making his first-team debut at Anfield.

The season finished with Liverpool beating Queen's Park Rangers to the title by one point and Southampton beating Manchester United in the FA Cup Final. Both the Liverpool A and B teams finished in second place in their respective Leagues, with Tommy scoring frequently for both as well as bagging nine for the reserves.

One evening, after a reserve game, Tommy noticed Bob Paisley talking to an American. His name was Al Miller and he was the first-team coach of NASL side the Dallas Tornadoes. He was interested in taking Tommy and another reserve team player, Kevin Kewley, to Dallas, and Paisley thought it might do the youngsters some good. Before long, Tommy and Kevin found themselves flying out to America; Tommy had never been anywhere like the US in his life.

The Tornadoes were owned by Lamar Hunt, a multi-millionaire and the son of an oil tycoon. Born in Texas in 1932, Hunt was initially involved in American football rather than soccer. He was the leading founder of the American Football League in 1960, which would evolve into the world-famous NFL in 1966. He was also responsible for coining the phrase 'Superbowl', named after his daughter's 'Super Ball', a popular toy in the summer of 1966. Hunt was at one time the owner of the Kansas City Chiefs and was also involved in establishing World Championship Tennis.

America was fast becoming the stomping ground for some of the biggest names in the game who were in the final years of their careers, and the good money was a bonus. The trend started in 1975 when the greatest player of all, the Brazilian striker Pelé, signed for the New York Cosmos for an astronomical fee of $4.5 million. He helped to turn the fortunes of the struggling NASL around. Soon, other teams were following suit in an attempt to keep up with the Cosmos. When George Best, Eusebio, Bobby Moore and Franz Beckenbauer arrived in America the crowds came flocking to see the stars. As their name became famous around the world, the New York Cosmos were used to playing in front of 70,000 spectators in the mid-1970s. Many of the imports were past their best (for example, Eusebio's knees had gone) but most managed to shine at the level they were playing at. The arrival of such players soon helped raise the quality of the football in the NASL, and before long it was common practice for European clubs to send youngsters out to America to play with the greats.

Everything was so much bigger stateside, including the food. A steak was as thick as your granny's doorstep back home in good old Liverpool. The differences between the two places were dramatic and took some getting used to. The American coaches ran their teams very differently. On a Friday evening everyone would head up to TGI Friday's, a chain of fast-food bars, where crazy things happened. There was a man up there who ran around in a gorilla suit and tried to get people to buy food and drink. Dallas was like a breath of fresh air, the whole place was alive and Tommy felt like he was on holiday.

The openness and the 'american way' was very appealing. When they were not training or playing they spent much of their spare time driving around in the sunshine discovering amazing people and places.

Tommy Tynan made his debut for the Dallas Tornadoes on 17 April 1976 against the Washington Diplomats. The Tornadoes won the game 1–0 and he came close to finding the net on a couple of occasions. They followed this with another 1–0 win against Bobby Moore's San Antonio Thunder and then they beat San Jose Earthquakes, with Tommy coming on as a sub. He scored his first goal against St Louis Stars on 6 June and Dallas won 2–0. Next came a win against Minnesota, but then the youngster found himself sidelined for the rest of the month after pulling ligaments in his knee. It was an injury that later flared up again during his time with Plymouth Argyle. He returned to action against Geoff Hurst's Seattle Sounders in July 1976 and responded by scoring in a 4–2 victory. They were then beaten 2–0 by Rochester Lancers on the 18th and followed this six days later with a 3–0 win against Portland Timbers. Jeff Borne scored all of the goals that day and he went on to end the season as top scorer for the Tornadoes with 16 goals in 24 games. He had been a fringe-player for First Division Derby County and was unable to hold down a regular position in the first team despite scoring goals. After a successful spell with the Tornadoes he returned to England to ply his trade with Crystal Palace. Looking back, Tommy has this to say about his American adventure:

'Bloody hell, it was like playing for Walt Disney. It was typical American glitz and glamour. They really didn't have a clue about things like diet, tactics or training – what I would call the

professionalism of the English game. I'd never been offered a steak during a pre-match meal before, but then again I'd never seen a bloke ride in on a horse pulling a hand stand before a match either!'

On 28 July 1976 the Ownby Stadium was packed. Pelé and the New York Cosmos were in town and everyone wanted to see the greatest centre-forward of all time. One of the Tornadoes' English players, Geoff Ley, had previously had the honour of marking Pelé during the previous season in his first game for the Cosmos, a season which had ended with Pelé bagging seven goals from 11 games. His fine form in 1976 brought a further 15 goals from 24 games. He signed off in 1977 with 17 from 31 appearances; it was the end of an era for the NASL and football and he retired without ever kicking a football in a competitive match for a European side.

Despite a brave effort from the Tornadoes, the Cosmos were far too strong. Tommy spent the whole match running and chasing balls, waiting for something to drop out of the air for him to get on the end of. The Cosmos went on to win 4–0. Chances were few and far between, and Tommy can still remember Pelé's commanding performance despite being only four years away from his 40th birthday. Everyone back home had seen the trickery and skill of the Brazilian team; they had ruined the dreams of the nation when they took the World Cup from England in 1970. For Tommy, to have been involved in such a game and to have played against Pelé was a true honour and the match remains one of the highlights of his footballing career. The problem for the youngster that day was the service; the Cosmos were so strong that he was not able to see enough of the ball to crack it into the back of the net. After the match Tommy shook hands with the greatest footballer who ever lived as the teams made their way off the pitch.

The New York Cosmos also had a former Italian international centre-forward called Giorgio Chinaglia playing for them at the time. Chinaglia was born in Italy but raised in Wales and got his first chance with Cardiff City before moving back to Italy to play for such teams as Inter Milan and Lazio. He also played 14 times for the Italian national side and scored four goals. Tommy remembers:

'There was a joke going around at the time that Chinaglia was part of the Mafia. When he was at the Cosmos he would turn up for training with Pelé in a helicopter, and all the Cosmos players would have to clear the pitch so the bloody thing could land! After the session, both men would get taken home the same way. Pelé was such a star over there that he even picked the US All-Star team that played once or twice a year and consisted of mainly British players.'

There were quite a number of big-name players who tried their luck in the NASL when Tommy was there. Geoff Hurst spent a season with the Seattle Sounders before returning home and in all competitions he notched up eight goals from 24 games. Chelsea legend Peter Osgood also spent a season in America playing for Philadelphia Fury and managed just one from 22 games. Although Tommy never played against Eusebio, 1976 proved to be an excellent year for the Portuguese star, who was capped 64 times for his country. After a disappointing start with the Boston Minutemen the previous season, he was transferred to the Toronto Metros and it was a move that saw him score more goals than Pelé that year, grabbing 18 from 25 games.

After the 4–0 defeat by the Cosmos, the Tornadoes suffered their second defeat on 7 August when they were beaten 3–2 by San Antonio Thunder. Next there was a win against San Diego before the Tornadoes faced Los Angeles Aztecs and George Best. They were beaten 4–1 by Best and his team, but they would avenge themselves by beating them 2–0 in the Play-offs. The Tornadoes finished the season in second position in the Southern Division and San Jose Earthquake won the League. LA Aztecs finished third, the Sounders fourth and San Diego Jaws finished bottom. Tommy created more goals than he scored throughout the summer and his season total, including the two Play-off matches, was 19 games and two goals. The Tornadoes won 12 and lost the other seven in what turned out to be a decent season. Behind top scorer Jeff Borne was Jim Ryan with nine goals. Kevin Kewley netted an impressive seven from 26. Tommy's last game for the Dallas Tornadoes was in a Play-off match against Southern League Champions San Jose Earthquake on 20 August, and they were beaten 2–0. Both Englishmen were on a plane home soon afterwards.

Tommy returned to action for Liverpool reserves in early September 1976, but he was no longer happy languishing in the second team when he knew he could be playing in stadiums full of people. The goals he had scored surely proved he had the ability to make it as a professional, but when he returned to Anfield things had changed. New players had been brought into the club by Bob Paisley, and it must have been a difficult time for him to make decisions as he had so much talent at his disposal and only 11 places to fill.

On the physical side of things, Tommy was looking sharp when he returned for training at the start of the 1976–77 season, and he felt good. Playing throughout the summer had given him and Kevin Kewley a bit more of an edge in terms of fitness. Despite all of these factors, Tommy left the club within a month of the new season beginning, moving to Sheffield Wednesday to ply his trade. There was, however, a final swansong as the reserves opened their Central League campaign against West Brom on 21 August and managed a 2–1 win away. They followed this four days later with another 2–1 home win against Leeds United and Tommy signed off for the Reds by scoring a hat-trick against Stoke City in a 6–0 rout at home on 7 September 1976.

However, would Tommy have made his debut for the Liverpool first team if Bill Shankly had stayed on past 1974 or if he had not been sold by Bob Paisley? It is an interesting question to which there can be no definite answer. With the quality of the first-team squad being so high there seemed to be no place for him in the first XI at the time. It is interesting to note that a couple of years later, while he was being interviewed, Paisley said that he had sold Tommy far too early and he regretted not giving him his chance in the Liverpool first team. Tommy was quite flattered when his former boss compared him to one of Liverpool's greatest players. He told the interviewer that Tommy had everything as a player apart from pace, very much like Kenny Dalglish.

> *'It's weird what Bob Paisley later said because at the time I think we were both starting to think the same way. I was getting older and I wasn't getting first-team football despite everything I was doing in the reserves.'*

The problem at Liverpool at the time, if you can call it that, was the lack of opportunity for the younger players. We have already mentioned Shankly's reliance on his first team, and if those players were fit they were rarely changed. Shankly's game was not a 'squad' game, he relied on the steel and guts of his first XI to see him through come rain or shine, and Paisley was the same. Unless your leg was broken in a tackle you got back up and played, and only if a player was out would there be a chance for someone else to step in. Despite the goals Tommy scored (he was top scorer in the reserves during the 1973–74 season) there were still reserve players ahead of him like Jimmy Case and Phil Boersma, who scored goals when given a run in the first team.

In terms of what was to come, Shankly left the club a little too soon. A couple of seasons after his departure it all came together for

Liverpool and they went on to win several European Cups. Bill had been forced to quit early due to his wife's ill health. The European Cup was the trophy that had always eluded him and it could not have been easy seeing Bob Paisley take the club that final step. Bill Shankly was a gentleman, however, and he would have been one of the first people to congratulate Paisley. If there was any jealousy or resentment on Bill's part it was not long-lasting, he was not the sort of man who held a grudge.

However, although Tommy was disappointed not to make his first-team debut for Liverpool, it had been one hell of a ride for the youngster, who was still at the beginning of a career that would see him score goals consistently for many clubs. Looking around him at the people he had grown up with, Tommy eventually realised how lucky he was to have learned from the best.

His move to Sheffield Wednesday came about when manager Len Ashurst made an offer. He had missed Tommy after a reserve match but returned to Anfield a few days later to talk to the youngster about signing for the club. After giving the offer some consideration, Tommy sat down with Ashurst and Paisley and they agreed a deal. Paisley knew how desperate the youngster was to play first-team football and Wednesday were a big club. The loan move to Dallas had landed Tommy further down the pecking order on his return, and Paisley knew how short a footballer's career was. The lad had put the ball in the back of the net on so many occasions that Paisley could not say no to him having the opportunity to play first-team football away from Anfield.

In September 1976, two months before his 21st birthday, Tommy signed for Sheffield Wednesday for £10,000. Although it is not possible to be 100 per cent accurate due to the incomplete records, he had amassed around 48 goals from roughly 86 games for the reserves without a chance to show the Kop how he could shine in the first team. His three goals against Stoke City turned out to be his only hat-trick for the Reds. He had scored two goals in a game on 11 occasions for the reserves and scored many goals for both the A and B teams. As he shook Len Ashurst's hand, he knew the move to Sheffield Wednesday was the right thing to do and the opportunity of a lifetime. Tommy knew that he had to leave Liverpool to further his career:

'Wednesday were a big club and it was a decent chance. Of course, I was gutted at leaving but time was ticking by. I think if Liverpool had been doing badly at the time, scraping relegation or something and I didn't get a chance then I'd have been more hurt. It wasn't Joe Bloggs and people like that keeping me out of the first team, it was people like Kevin Keegan. Some of the best players in the world were there at the time and Liverpool's team were pretty unstoppable.'

Chapter 7
Sheffield Wednesday

Sheffield Wednesday have always been regarded as one of the 'big clubs' and enjoy a fierce rivalry with neighbours Sheffield United, the 'other' club from a city best known for its steel industry. Wednesday became members of Division One back in 1892 when the fledgling Football League was expanded to 16 teams. Instead of starting their League career alongside United in Division Two, Wednesday were elected to Division One where they stayed until 1899. Their first taste of promotion happened 12 months later when they returned to the top flight after relegation and they won their first two League titles back-to-back in 1903 and 1904 when they were known simply as 'The Wednesday'. It was not until 1930 that the 'Sheffield' part was added to their name and they started the season as League Champions once again.

It is somewhat ironic that the last team Tommy played against for Liverpool reserves before going to America was Sheffield Wednesday. Sheffield was not an unfamiliar place to Tommy, as he had played at Hillsborough on a couple of occasions and his new lodgings, which he shared with three other youngsters, were just around the corner.

Len Ashurst had seen something special in Tommy, but he was still taking a gamble on him despite the goals he had scored for Liverpool reserves because he had not really proved himself at first-team level. Len had played for Sunderland for many years and his major strength as a manager was his ability to come in to a club and sort things out. His type of training was fitness-based and he had a talent for implementing new tactical systems. Despite the fact that Tommy had only played six full-team matches in England, and scored two while on loan at Swansea, he went straight into the first team for the match at Swindon Town on 11 September 1976. Swindon won the match 5–2, but he scored his first goal for the Owls that day in front of a crowd of 9,000. His second came against Chesterfield at Hillsborough in his very next match as Wednesday took all of the points in a 4–1 win. By the time he had made his 10th League appearance (his fourth for Wednesday) against Lincoln City in a one-all draw at Sincil Bank, he had notched up four League goals. On 20 November, three days after his 21st birthday, Tommy made his FA Cup debut and scored against Stockport in a 2–0 win in the first round. As 1976 drew to a close Wednesday were not exactly setting the division alight but the acquisition of players like Bobby Hope, Dennis Leahman and Geoff Johnson from Man City were adding quality to the mix. By the new year Tommy had netted 10 of the 15 goals he went on to score that season, linking up with Roger Wilde and Bobby Hope, whom he had played with in America. On 6 November 1976 Wednesday beat Bury away from home 3–1, with Tommy scoring two in a competitive match for the very first time. His second brace came two games later as they beat Peterborough United 2–1 away from home. In terms of goals, it had been quite a lucrative start to his first full season in League football.

1977 was the year that George Lucas launched the film *Star Wars* to worldwide acclaim and John Travolta kick-started the 'disco' craze when he starred in *Saturday Night Fever*. *The Krypton Factor* was making its television debut while Paul McCartney and his band, Wings, were hanging about at number one in the pop charts for nine weeks with the hit single *Mull of Kintyre*. In Miami, on 19 January, snow fell for the only time in recorded history and it proved to be a difficult month for Tommy too as Wednesday limped on. They started the year with draws against Grimsby and Brighton before being beaten away from home by Mansfield Town. On the 27th the Sex Pistols were sacked by EMI and 16 days later Tommy hit his third brace in a 3–0 win against Portsmouth. By 1 March the 21-year-old had netted 14 goals. Wednesday were knocked out in the second round of both domestic Cups and there was not much for the fans to cheer about. However, Tommy's performances showed his commitment along with his ability. Len Ashurst had already seen a good return on the money the club had spent as Tommy was involved in 43 of the 50 League and Cup games Wednesday played that season as they finished eighth in Division Three and missed out on promotion once again.

At Anfield the majority of media interest focused on the first team and what they had achieved. However, reports about reserve-team matches and Tommy's endeavours in front of goal filtered through to scouts and managers, and the media attention he was now about to receive at Wednesday was like nothing he had ever experienced before. He had seen the razzmatazz of America and enjoyed some good write-ups in the Welsh Press during his time at Swansea City, but this was something else.

As a Liverpool youth player Tommy was able to spend time around the first team and the media circus that followed them. This allowed him to experience first-hand what the limelight was like and such early encounters helped him to deal with similar events in his own future. When Plymouth beat Derby in 1984 and were drawn against Watford in the semi-finals of the FA Cup, everyone wanted to know about the Devon team and their star striker and Tommy experienced his own taste of fame. The national press even ran the headline 'Tommy Gun' and dressed him as a 1930s mobster brandishing a gun. Tommy had seen players like Kevin Keegan deal with the media. He had always been a gentleman and would be firm but fair, taking the time to answer questions before going about his business and Tommy had learned much from Shankly and others, which helped to inspire and motivate him to become better in front of the camera as well as on the pitch. He never forgot his manners whether he was playing in some bleak Eastern bloc country in a European match or pitting his wits against the best in America.

There have, of course, been times when Tommy has lost his cool and all logic and reason has flown out of the window. There have also been occasions when he was shown the red card, but this was never commonplace during his career. While he could never be described as a troublemaker, Tommy was not afraid to stand up for what he believed to be right. There were incidents, like the Torquay United card school, which ended up in the newspapers (such matters will be discussed later in this book) but the majority of publicity Tommy received throughout his career was positive, such as the reaction to his four goals against Blackburn Rovers on 5 November 1988. The most important thing to remember about Tommy's career is that he was a great goalscorer and he did it at every level he had the chance to play at. Perhaps it was a little bit of the Bill Shankly never-say-die attitude instilled in him, or the skills he had learned growing up on Liverpudlian council estates in the 1950s and 1960s that made him so great. Whatever it was that gave him that magic touch in front of goal is baffling to the man himself, and sitting down with him trying to single out and analyze the skill revealed nothing further. Tommy Tynan was a natural and he just loved to score goals – and that was that!

Sheffield Wednesday were big enough to make headline news and whenever a player was out in public they had to bear in mind that they were representing the club. Tommy learned about the media interest surrounding the team quite quickly:

'One night we were all in a nightclub having a few drinks and a bit of a laugh. And then, one of the players, I'm not gonna say who, but, he was pretty bloody pissed. Anyway, he ended up climbing up on the table, dropping his trousers and showing his arse. I can promise you it was absolutely nothing to do with me, but

before I know it I'm roped in on it. It was a pretty serious offence back then and this player actually got the boot from Wednesday for what happened. Anyway, the next day I went into training and a few of the bodies are looking at me a bit serious like. It only turns out that my name has been given as the perpetrator and I was nothing to do with it. Luckily, a few of the lads and a couple of the others who were there with me actually vouched for me and I was okay.'

The stunt caused a bit of a stir but Tommy learnt a valuable lesson. Whatever any of the Wednesday lads did was news. If they had been spotted in the local supermarket, let alone in the pub, the process of 'chinese whispers' would generate a new tale for the rumour-merchants. If a player was seen with a few beers inside him after a match he was an open target for allegations and abuse. Although the media are quicker to jump on the footballers of today, life could be made a living hell even back then.

Discipline is one of the key ingredients in the running of a football team; from the self-discipline of the individual player out in the community to the discipline instilled by the board of directors, the manager and the coaching staff. There have, of course, been times on and off the pitch when Tommy has fallen foul of a referee or a manager, and there were times he was sent off, but it was incidents like the one above that made him sit up and think. Tommy says:

'Okay, I had my fair share of trouble along the way but it's because I didn't want anyone to take the mick, especially in the later stages of my career when I'd seen it all before. That night in the club when my mate dropped his trousers was a shock, and I'm not just talking about the colour of his pants. It was then that I realised that people were taking notice of what we were doing when we were off the pitch as well!'

After the disappointment of the 1976–77 season many people felt Len Ashurst's days were numbered. Wednesday had always been one of those clubs expected to be in the top flight and the fan base was massive. Whenever Wednesday were relegated a 'miracle cure' was immediately sought for a swift return and pressure put on the manager to get it right. When the unthinkable occurred and Wednesday went down into the old Third Division, patience was a little thin on the ground. Missing out on promotion at the end of the 1976–77 season meant that results had to improve immediately.

At Anfield Liverpool were on their way to winning their 10th League title, and finished the season on 57 points, one more than second-placed Manchester City. The red half of Manchester denied Liverpool their first League and Cup double by beating them 2–1 in the FA Cup Final, with goals coming from Pearson and Greenhoff for United, Jimmy Case getting the consolation for the Merseysiders. Liverpool would have to wait until 1986 for their first League and FA Cup double. Elsewhere, Aston Villa beat Everton 3–2 after extra-time in the second replay to lift the 1977 League Cup, with two goals coming from future manager Brian Little. In total they had played more than five hours and 30 minutes of football before the sides could be separated. Tottenham, who did the double themselves in 1961, were relegated from the top flight for the first time since 1935 and Workington slipped out of Division Four and into non-League obscurity.

This was also the year Plymouth Argyle were relegated from Division Two, finishing second from bottom with just 32 points. After seven seasons in Division Three, goals from Paul Mariner and Billy Rafferty had helped Argyle to promotion in 1975, but after two seasons in the second tier they found themselves back where they had started, winning just eight League matches all season. Wednesday's rivals, Sheffield United, finished mid-table in Division Two after relegation from the top flight two seasons earlier. If the Wednesday fans thought things were bad, then United were a club at crisis point. They fell into the old Fourth Division in 1981, only to be promoted as champions a season later. When Wednesday returned to the top flight in 1984 as runners-up to Chelsea, it was the end of a 14-year period without top-flight football and the first time in nine years that a Sheffield team had played in the First Division. Sheffield United did not see top-flight action again until 1990.

Like the season before, Wednesday started the 1977–78 season against Swindon Town, and Tommy scored once again. This time the match was at home on 20 August and it ended 1–1. Things did not improve, however, and in Len Ashurst's final 10 League games Wednesday lost five and drew five. Looking back on Wednesday's slump in form, Tommy says:

> *'I think at that point Len desperately needed to change things around, but he was being too loyal to his players who weren't giving anything back. They were letting him down on the pitch.'*

Len was finally sacked after a 2–1 defeat at Preston on 4 November 1977. Tommy had managed three goals, one against Swindon on the opening day, one against Chester City on 14 September and one against Portsmouth in a two-all draw at Fratton Park on 10 October. He had also managed three in the League Cup, which gave him a respectable total of six from 14 matches.

Despite the goals and the fact that Wednesday were propping up the Third Division, Len opted to leave Tommy out for the match at Preston. Tommy was fuming so he decided to go and have a word with Len:

> *'Len had been changing the team about and the results were not improving, despite the arrival of quite a few new players. I wasn't happy because I had scored nearly half of Wednesday's goals, I was fit and I was chomping at the bit. I think we had only scored four*

times in the opening nine League matches, and we had banged in another 13 in the League Cup. I was keen to get in there and I suppose I was just frustrated. I asked him why he had left me out of the team and he gave me a right earful. He told me that he was manager and he was the one who made the decisions. I told him that he was showing too much loyalty to players who were not pulling their weight and that those players would get him the sack. For example, bloody Shrewsbury had beaten us at Hillsborough, can you imagine that? We had also lost to some really rubbish teams that year and I just wasn't happy about being left out, that's all I was trying to say. After that he told me to get out of his office, and if I didn't like it I knew what I could do. He was the manager and he knew what was best for the club, it was as simple as that.'

Despite the disagreement there was mutual respect between the two men and the argument was not long-lasting, despite Len's sacking. This was not the last time they would not see eye to eye. At Wednesday, disagreement with Tony Toms did not help Tommy's situation either. The squad were in the gym one day and Toms was explaining the basics of a multi-gym, even though all the players knew how to use the machines. Tommy told Toms that he felt they were wasting time when they could already be training and he was told to leave.

The Preston defeat in November signalled the end of Len Ashurst's reign as manager. Wednesday brought in their shortest serving manager, Ken Knighton, who took charge for the Chesterfield match four days later. The team beat Chesterfield 1–0 at home, with Tommy scoring the only goal. It was the first League game he had played in which Wednesday had won that season. They had beaten Fourth Division Doncaster Rovers over two legs in the League Cup and they followed this in the second round by knocking out Second Division Blackpool, but they had not won in the League. After the game,

Tommy noticed Len Ashurst up in the stand. It had been less than a week since he had thrown Tommy out of his office and now he was out of a job. Never one to hold a grudge, Tommy went up into the stand after the match to see him. Len was a true gentleman and on seeing Tommy he shook his hand and told him that he had been right about what he had said. Len's loyalty to his underachieving players had finally got him the sack and he was big enough to admit it. Even today, whenever anybody asks Tommy who inspired him throughout his career, Len Ashurst's name always comes up and it is not difficult to understand why.

Chapter 8
Enter Jack Charlton

In October 1977 Jack Charlton took over at Sheffield Wednesday. Everybody has heard of the Charlton brothers. Born in Ashington, Northumbria, Jack came into the world first on 8 May 1935 and then Bobby followed on 11 October 1937. At first Bobby overshadowed Jack on his way to becoming a Manchester United legend, but John 'Jack' Charlton soon became an integral part of the Leeds United team that Don Revie built his defence around. Jack was at first offered an apprenticeship at Leeds and turned pro in 1952 at the age of 17. He made his senior debut in April 1953 and was a first-team regular within two years. He married Pat on 16 January 1958, a month before his brother (who was his best man) was involved in the Munich air disaster. And, of course, there was that famous day in 1966 when England won the World Cup at Wembley and both brothers played a key role. They share a famous footballing uncle, Jackie Milburn, and are both remembered for the outstanding contribution they made to their respective clubs and to their country.

Jack was on national service when his brother Bobby first started to hit the headlines, but he was soon spotted playing central-defence at amateur level. By then he had been working in a coal mine and had quit his job to apply for the police force. Unfortunately, the interview for the police was on the same day as his Leeds trial, which was a game that Jack could not miss. The early 1950s Leeds United team struggled in Division Two, but a side built around John Charles were too good to languish in the Second Division for long. They were promoted as runners-up to Sheffield Wednesday in 1956 under Raich Carter before

Don Revie took the reins in 1961. As a player, Jack had not always seen eye to eye with Revie and he feared for his place when he took over as manager. Manchester United and Liverpool could not afford his asking price so Jack and Don made amends and the team went on to great things. The last piece of the jigsaw was the emergence of Norman Hunter from the youth set-up whom Tommy was later to play under at Rotherham United. At Leeds Jack went on to win one League title and they were runners-up on five occasions as well as winning the FA Cup, the League Cup and the Fairs Cup. When he finally retired at the age of 38, he had played 773 games and scored 96 goals, occasionally appearing as a makeshift centre-forward.

The season prior to Tommy's arrival at Hillsborough Sheffield Wednesday finished in 20th position in Division Three. It was their worst season to date, nothing clicked and the club had no money. Previously, their darkest days had been either side of World War Two when they struggled in the Second Division for a few seasons before regaining their status as a First Division team. After relegation once again in 1970, it took them 14 seasons to return to the top, spending five years in what was then the Third Division. After Len Ashurst's dismal start to the 1977–78 campaign it was hoped things would improve under a new manager and that a serious promotion challenge could be mounted. It took the incoming Jack Charlton another three and a half seasons to transform his team and the club won promotion in 1980 as they finished third.

Jack's first game in charge ended in a 2–1 defeat away to Exeter City on 12 October, and it was clear a miracle cure was not imminent. Wednesday finished in 14th position that year but Tommy managed to improve on his tally of 15 from the previous season, netting 21 in all competitions. His first League goal under Jack came at the Racecourse Ground on 15 October, where he scored Wednesday's only goal as they held Wrexham to a draw. It is fair to say that Tommy had mixed feelings about his new boss:

'Jack was lovely. It's true that we didn't see eye to eye over tactics but he was smashing. You wouldn't believe he was a World Cup winner. I can remember one day when he picked a load of his players up in a van and took us shooting in some woodlands near his mother's home. He was very laid back, maybe a little bit too laid back for me. It was not what I'd been used to at Liverpool or under Len.'

The first time Tommy was on a winning side under Jack was on 22 October when they beat Lincoln City 2–0 at home, and it was at this match that Tommy had an overwhelming experience. It was totally unexpected and made him think about the power of the crowd in a brand new way. He felt he had put in a solid performance, as did all of the team, and Wednesday had won 2–0, and although he had not scored the team worked as it should, surging forward and defending as a collective. As the battle wore on, the players left the pitch with the points and Tommy noticed that the home supporters were standing and clapping after witnessing an excellent game of football. He naturally assumed that the standing ovation was for the team but in fact it had been for him. Two games later he was playing the 60th League game of his career against Carlisle United, and he scored again in a 3–1 win on 5 November.

Centre-forwards of Tommy's calibre are ultimately judged by the goals they score, so despite a solid performance, he had not realised just how well he had played. Fans love to see the star centre-forward weaving the ball through the opposition defence and scoring the winner, but when the chips are down they like to see players rolling up their sleeves and pitching in. When Tommy realised that thousands of people were standing and applauding his performance, he must have felt like the lead singer in a large rock band being cheered towards an encore. His performance earned him the Man of the Match award and his name was splashed across the pages of the sports Press.

A barren spell began as Jack Charlton's honeymoon period ended. In the next five games Tommy was involved in, Wednesday lost four and drew one with Tommy scoring once. In the FA Cup after a first-round win at Hillsborough against Bury, they were beaten 1–0 by non-League side Wigan Athletic. Despite the indifferent results, it was soon apparent that things really were starting to change. Jack liked playing a lone striker up front, which was something Tommy hated and was the reason he eventually left Sheffield Wednesday. In another experiment, goalscoring centre-forward Roger Wilde was played in midfield. Tommy liked to play alongside another centre-forward to be at his predatory best. With another striker to hold the ball up and make the passes, he always scored goals.

By Saturday 5 November Wednesday had managed to pull away from the bottom of the League to the dizzy heights of 23rd. Tommy scored at Carlisle that day as they registered a first away win in the League with a 3–1 victory. They only managed one more point through November and most of December, and Tommy scored Wednesday's only goal during a 3–1 defeat at Tranmere on Boxing Day. However, fortunes were about to improve for the club. Tommy scored again on the 27th as they beat Rotherham 1–0 and they recorded the same result on New Year's Eve against Hereford, but, despite these victories, they remained in 23rd position with just 17 points from 23 League games. As Jack Charlton searched for the results to move them away from the relegation zone the new year started with disaster as an Air India Boeing 747 exploded in Bombay on 1 January.

On 2 January Wednesday lost 1–0 at Carlisle as their troubles continued. Tommy continued to make as many goalscoring opportunities as he could, despite his increasing unhappiness. Mark Smith, now a youth-team coach at Wednesday, was Tommy's boot boy at the time, and he recalls how hard he worked during training. Smith, who was a useful defender and good in the air, also plied his trade with Plymouth as well as the England Under-21 team, recalls how annoyed Tommy would get when he missed the target, and that was just during training. Tommy always wanted to put the ball in the back of the net and it must have been frustrating being left up front on his own. If Tommy did get annoyed it was usually with himself, and Smith remembers he was good with the younger players; there was no feeling of 'us and them', he treated the youngsters no differently from the senior professionals and he always gave Smith a few extra quid at Christmas for cleaning his boots. Smith also remembers how he helped both himself and his wife Kim settle in the Plymouth area when he signed for Plymouth for a then record fee of £170,000 in 1987. Despite Tommy's mounting frustrations at the time, we must remember that he still finished the season as top scorer with 21 goals. How many more could he have scored if Jack Charlton had played two up front more regularly?

On 14 February Leon Spinks won the World Heavyweight title, beating Muhammad Ali and inflicting his first defeat, while Wednesday battled on through the month. Tommy scored his 10th League goal during a 3–1 win at Hillsborough against a soon to be relegated Port Vale team on the 11th, before Wednesday recorded defeats against Peterborough, Portsmouth and Shrewsbury. March brought a vast improvement as Wednesday finally became upwardly mobile. Their only defeat of the month was at Lincoln on the 18th. On the 22nd a solitary penalty from Robertson at Old Trafford in front of 54,000 saw Nottingham Forest beat Liverpool in the League Cup Final replay. On the 25th Oxford won the boat race when the Cambridge boat sank a mile from the finish.

By 1 April Wednesday were in 16th position in the table, amassing 36 points from 38 games. During their final nine (eight of which Tommy was involved in) they managed four wins, four draws and lost 2–1 at Gillingham on the 15th. The final game of the season took place on 3 May and ended in a 2–1 win against Wrexham at

Hillsborough, and Tommy ended the season with another goal. Luckily there was no pitch invasion, but on the same day, during a test match in Jamaica between the West Indies and Australia, police fired over spectators after they invaded the pitch!

On 6 May Ipswich won the FA Cup for the only time, beating Arsenal, and Nottingham Forest won the League for the very first time. It was a poor season for Manchester United as they finished 10th in the League behind lesser teams such as arch-rivals Manchester City. Tottenham were promoted back into the First Division in 1978 after finishing bottom the year before and Liverpool beat FC Bruges at Wembley to lift the European Cup once again. In Division Three, Wednesday, Lincoln, Plymouth and Rotherham all finished in the bottom half as Watford gained promotion from the Fourth Division in only their third League season. It was the beginning of a meteoric rise through the Leagues for the Hornets, and by 1982 they would find themselves mixing it with the big boys, finishing as runners-up to Liverpool in the League a year later. For Tommy it was the beginning of the end of his time at Sheffield Wednesday.

Chapter 9
Out of the Door and Northwards

The 1977–78 season failed to live up to expectations. During the previous five seasons Wednesday fans had watched their team slip out of the second tier and now they were just about keeping their heads above water in the Third Division. There was to be no light at the end of the tunnel for another two seasons, but it was not all doom and gloom, as despite their lowly finish they had conceded fewer goals than the season before and they now looked capable of scoring. The shape of the team was not the only thing Jack had changed, as training was now also very different. The intense fitness regime of Len Ashurst gave way to more tactically based training. Tony Toms was still working on the fitness and conditioning of the players, but Jack's approach was rather more laid back. Toms, who used to be a physical training instructor in the army, must have found it interesting to compare the training methods of Ashurst and Charlton. Toms would be the first to admit that he did not know a lot about football, but what he knew about conditioning and fitness was invaluable. Tommy makes an interesting comparison between the two regimes. He believes that if you could draw 50 per cent of the training methods from both Charlton and Ashurst and put them together you would end up with a near perfect regime. He found Ashurst's pre-season tough and there was no being eased back into things, it was straight in from day one. Jack liked to talk tactics and wanted to expand a player's awareness of the game and what was going on around him.

Things did not feel so rigid under Jack, but that was not necessarily a good thing. Club discipline is instilled and enforced by the manager and his coaching staff, and while it can be good for the manager to be one of the lads it is also good to know where to draw the line. Most players call the manager 'Boss' or 'Gaffer' or something similar. Jack Charlton wanted to be known as 'Jack', and this was something Tommy and many of the players could not get used to. If a young player had addressed Bill Shankly in such a manner he would have received a harsh dressing down for his troubles. Although it may seem to be a petty complaint, in a football environment communication and the precision of information is of paramount importance. Any erosion of such a relationship is detrimental to the overall effect of the team. You would never hear a corporal calling a brigadier 'mate' or a junior nurse call matron 'love', and the same is true in the world of football. Tommy says:

> 'As I said before, Jack was just a bit too laid back, I think players need the discipline, the professional distance and a hierarchy.'

Jack continued to play Tommy up front as a lone striker and the role was not one he enjoyed. As a target man, Tommy was no longer enjoying his football and felt he was running and chasing balls all match with little effect. Running for 90 minutes solid was draining, but he still managed 15 goals from the 50 matches he played for Jack. Jack himself was also becoming a little bit of a problem off the pitch for Tommy. On the pitch the results had started to improve. After a bad spell of five games without a win, Wednesday managed five wins from the next seven, and Tommy added two more to his tally. A run of three wins in a row was ended by Peterborough on 22 February 1978 at their ground. Jack was not happy at losing and even though nobody ever went to an extreme during Tommy's time at the club, after the trouser-dropping stunt, he banned the players from going out that night:

> *'I was living in digs near Hillsborough when I first met my Elaine. She was working in a nightclub called Josephine's in the centre of Sheffield, which was owned by Dave Allen, who was later the chairman of Sheffield Wednesday. Although we were all banned by Jack from going out that night, he did say to me that it would be okay to pop into the club to tell Elaine that I could not stay, as long as I didn't stop for a drink. She was fine with it and agreed to meet up after work to go back to her place. There was no training the next day and I often stayed over at hers when I didn't have to get up early. I was living with another player called Hughie Dowd at the time, so if one of us wanted to have our girlfriend over we usually made some kind of arrangement so that we could have the place to ourselves, and I agreed to stay over at Elaine's that night. When I returned to the lodgings the next day, Hughie looked white. He said that Jack and Tony had called in at 1am to see if I was there and Jack had put two and two together and blown his top, believing I had defied his instructions and gone out drinking.'*

After that the relationship soured somewhat and Tommy knew he wanted out of Sheffield Wednesday. It was not just the fact that he was trying to run Tommy's private life, but he was also unhappy with the systems Jack was playing out on the park. Instead of letting it get to him, Tommy tried to be constructive and soon went on the transfer list. The best way to get noticed was to just get his head down and play.

Both Tommy and Elaine had been married before and Elaine had two young children – Tammy, who was born 1971, and Keeley, who was born in 1973. Soon they were keen to set up house as a family.

He had originally asked her out on behalf of another player, but Elaine was not interested and asked to go out with Tommy instead. She knew who Tommy was, although when the players were on a night out they would not tell anyone they were footballers, despite the fact that their cover story (they told people they were plumbers) was impossible to believe when their faces were plastered across the newspapers and television!

Back then there were no agents to do deals like there are today and after receiving Elaine's support Tommy did all of his own negotiating. He had never had to do this before, as Paisley had sorted his move out to Wednesday and in retrospect he can appreciate how naive he really was. He had wanted a decent deal in the region of £10,000 to go to a club with a lesser reputation than Wednesday. Willie Bell, manager of Lincoln City, was offering £5,000 so they split the difference and he signed for £7,500 in three instalments over the course of the contract, with a wage of £145 a week plus a win bonus. After some haggling, Tommy got £2,500 up front. The money was not actually part of his £33,000 transfer fee and he effectively signed for Lincoln City for nothing!

Tony Toms later went on record stating that Tommy left Hillsborough because of him, but this simply was not the case. Willie Bell came in with a £25,000 offer and a deal was done. Despite the fact Tommy had been voted Player of the Year and scored 21 goals the year before, Jack did not want the aggravation and a deal was done within two weeks. Tommy discussed the idea of a move with Elaine towards the end of 1977 and she agreed to support his decision. Tommy had spoken to Jack about how he felt and that he was unhappy playing up front on his own, but his words had fallen on deaf ears. Jack wanted to play the game his way and Tommy was experienced enough to accept it.

There were many good times under Jack and he certainly had the ability to make people laugh. If there had been another forward-thinking player in the starting XI who could hold the ball up and create opportunities, Tommy may have enjoyed many more seasons with Wednesday. Who knows, he may well have been around in 1984 when they were promoted back into the top flight. Although teams of today often play with just one centre-forward, it was just not the done thing back in 1978. Tommy found it rather ironic that after his departure Jack played more regularly with two up front. If he had known that this was going to happen he would have stayed on at Hillsborough. As it was, he was not looking forward to another season playing this way, chasing balls with little effect. When Willie Bell came along it was a case of it being the right time for a move and Lincoln was not a million miles away from Sheffield. There was an optimistic mood at the club. Little did he know how soon things would change. His record spoke for itself by the time he left Wednesday. He had scored a total of 38 goals in 101 games.

As the season ended Tommy was delighted when Liverpool won the European Cup again and it was all thanks to a goal from Kenny Dalglish, who had been brought in to replace Kevin Keegan when he was sold to SV Hamburg. On 25 June Argentina beat Holland 3–1 after extra-time to lift the 1978 World Cup, with the two winning goals coming from Mario Kempes. After the summer and still being a Wednesday player, Tommy reported back for pre-season training, waiting for the move to happen.

Sheffield Wednesday played their first match of the season at Belle Vue on the 12th and they beat Doncaster 1–0 in the first leg of the first round of the League Cup. After drawing on aggregate after the second leg, a replay was played and Wednesday finally made it into the second round. Their League campaign started at Peterborough on 12 August and they were soundly beaten by two goals to nil. A week later they could only manage a 0–0 draw against Colchester at home and it looked as if Wednesday were in for another hard slog. On the 30th they travelled to Villa Park to face Aston Villa in the second round of the League Cup. Villa were an up-and-coming team who went on to win the League title in 1981 and lift the European Cup a year later. After giving a good account of themselves, Wednesday maintained the respect of their First Division opponents and were only beaten 1–0. On 2 September they beat Lincoln City at Sincil Bank and Tommy scored his last goal in blue and white against the team he would soon be playing for. The day before Muhammad Ali beat Leon Spinks to regain his heavyweight title on 17 September, Wednesday drew at Mansfield. It was plain for all to see that they were not exactly setting the League alight.

Chapter 10
Three Clubs in
One Season

Lincoln City officially started life in 1884 as an amateur club, but a team had been playing at John O'Gaunts since the 1860s. In 1885 they moved to their current ground at Sincil Bank and reached the last 16 of the FA Cup in 1890. They were knocked out of the competition by the then Cup holders, Preston North End. A year later they turned professional and were original members of Division Two in 1892–93, when they finished ninth. Nicknamed the Imps, they stayed in this League without ever really impressing until 1908 when they finished bottom with just 21 points. Their best season to date was the 1901–02 season when they finished fifth in Division Two. In 1911 they were promoted to the second tier again, finished bottom and dropped out of the League once more. They were back for another go in 1912–13, but just as they were getting into it football was suspended as World War One began. With the creation of Division Three North in 1921, Lincoln had yet another crack at it and they ambled along until the next round of hostilities began in 1939. A fire destroyed the South Park Stand and the offices during the 1929–30 season, and although the stand was rebuilt their early club records were lost forever.

After the war, and up to Tommy's arrival and beyond, the side were, on the whole, unremarkable, spending most of their time in the bottom two divisions with the exception of a couple of seasons in the 1930s, the late 1950s and early 1960s.

For Tommy the move to Lincoln was a disaster from the off, as not only was there no transfer fee but the manager, Willie Bell, did not live up to Tommy's expectations. When he had courted the young centre-forward for his signature, he had told him that the Imps were up-and-coming and they were building for the future. Unbeknown to Tommy, Bell was a very religious man and within three weeks he left the club to become an Evangelist preacher in the US, which, by his own admission, left Tommy in a mess.

> *'I was gutted. There were a few clubs who were interested in me, I'd been Player of the Year at Wednesday and Lincoln were a lot smaller. Anyway, Bell gave me all the old flannel about how progressive Lincoln were, what plans they had for the future and he pretty much sold it to me. Anyway, no sooner did I arrive, he went off to America and I was back in the wilderness again.'*

Tommy had signed for Lincoln in October 1978, and by February 1979 he was on his way south, signing for Newport County.

The 1978–79 season saw Tommy play for three clubs, and little did he know that he was at the start of one of the worst periods he would experience as a professional footballer. It was a very unsettled time for the youngster, who was still living in Sheffield with his partner Elaine and unable to drive. Young goalkeeper Chris Turner (who earned his great reputation at Sheffield Wednesday and Manchester United) gave Tommy a lift to the club every day, but the journey was daunting.

Tommy was due to make his debut for Lincoln at Blackpool, and when he got to the ground he made straight for the dressing room with the rest of the team. He remembers that at around 2pm he was just about to get changed when Bell turned up and told him he would not be playing. The club secretary had phoned him and told him that the FA had not received Tommy's registration papers in time, so he ended up travelling to Blackpool for nothing. His real debut came at home against Colchester United and the match ended goalless. Bell's team were then thumped 4–2 at Gillingham, and in Tommy's last game (his 100th League match) they were hammered 3–0 by Swindon Town in front of their home fans. Things went from bad to worse and at the end of the day he had the long, drawn out journey back home to Sheffield. They travelled up and down the motorway in all types of weather. Sometimes it could be icy and treacherous, and other times the journey could be slow and arduous. The spray from the thundering juggernauts made visibility virtually zero on really bad days.

As 1978 ended, Nottingham Forest were still making waves in the First Division thanks to Brian Clough – and Tommy felt a million miles away from success. Liverpool were looking to regain the League title from Forest, who were not able to sustain their League challenge and finished eight points behind Liverpool at the end of the 1978–79 season.

The year 1979 began with strike action. First it was the lorry drivers, then the rail workers and even the grave diggers in Liverpool had had enough and downed picks for a while. Sid Vicious, once of the Sex Pistols, was found dead due to a heroin overdose in a hotel room in New York and Margaret Thatcher was on her way in. In May that year milk went up to 15p a pint, while Ipswich Town defeated Arsenal in the FA Cup Final.

After Willie Bell had left for America, Colin Murphy was installed as the new manager at Lincoln. Murphy was a well respected manager who liked to play a physical style of football, but he did not like pretty football and he was even less keen on pretty footballers. He would not be the only manager Tommy would meet with this philosophy. He believed that in the lower Leagues you needed strength to get you out of trouble and all the fancy stuff should be left to the big teams and their stars. This was the final straw for Tommy and the push he needed to make the decision to move. He found Murphy's training hard mentally as well as physically, and it drained him, although he will be the first to admit that he lacked a little bit of fitness at that point in his career. It would take Len Ashurst's strict, but not so physical, training methods to get him back to his best. Not the biggest of men, Tommy can remember how Murphy almost kicked in the door to the changing rooms when he first addressed the team, and from then on things changed for the worse for him.

> *'Let's just say me and Colin Murphy had a different way of looking at the game. He saw me as a fancy player, more of a commodity. His idea was to get down to hard work and not play fancy football and that was it really.'*

In his first six matches in charge, Murphy picked up just three points, and still Tommy had not played in a winning Lincoln team. They managed a point when he returned to Hillsborough in a goalless draw and they hung on for a point against Plymouth Argyle in a thrilling 3–3 draw at Home Park. In his final game for the Imps Tommy found himself on the winning side at last as they took three points away at Peterborough, but he was just glad that the nightmare was finally over.

In total Tommy played nine times for Lincoln City and scored one goal in a stint that started in October 1978 and ended in February 1979. He also played six games for the reserves and scored 18 goals. Lincoln finished bottom in 1979 with only 25 points; they would have needed another 12 to avoid the drop so they were not even close. They managed just seven wins in the League all season and were beaten 28 times. To make things worse, they conceded 88 goals and scored a paltry 44. Thankfully, Tommy was away from the club by the time they were relegated.

Murphy's second season in charge at Lincoln turned out to be better, but Tommy had found his stride at Newport by then. His Lincoln team were just a little off the pace and finished in seventh place and seven points away from Portsmouth, who grabbed the last promotion place. It was not until 1981 that the Imps finally returned to Division Three, finishing as runners-up to Southend United. Lenny Lawrence was Murphy's assistant, and a few seasons after Tommy had left, while he was at Newport, he had a chat with him after a match. He was at Newport doing a bit of scouting, and he told Tommy how he had approached Colin Murphy and told him he had made a mistake selling him, and that all he needed to do was get him fit.

Tommy's move away from Lincoln City came about when he heard that his former manager, Len Ashurst, was keen to take him to his new club Newport County. The £25,000 transfer was, at the time, a record for the Welsh club and Tommy was offered a similar deal to what he was getting at Lincoln. He told Murphy that because it was Len who was making the offer he would be interested in listening, but he would have to speak to Elaine before making a final decision. Despite all the travelling and the trouble Tommy was having, he would still have to consider how she felt, but Elaine left the decision up to him. The next day Murphy drove Tommy down to Newport, and he could not believe just how far it was. He was unsure if Elaine would take to being this far away from her family and friends, and his initial reaction was that the move would not be good for him. However, he soon changed his mind and before long he was very impressed with Newport and what Len had to say.

Colin Murphy and Len Ashurst sat down and agreed the fee, with Tommy picking up £160 per week along with a nice win bonus. They also agreed a similar deal of £7,500 paid out in three lump sums to him, as well as a relocation fee. This relocation fee covered the cost of solicitors, removals and carpets and was considered as starting out money. On this occasion these costs amounted to £2,500 and so Tommy had a decent amount left over. In the modern game relocation fees for players can be well over £100,000, but for the late 1970s what he received was a pretty decent sum. The travelling to and from Sheffield was soon over, and within six months Tommy and his family had their own flat. It was another new chapter and Tommy could not wait for it to begin.

Chapter 11
Into the Valleys

It is true that the original Newport County Football Club escaped relegation many times. So many times, in fact, it should have been curtains for them, but again and again they were saved at the 11th hour, until the gates were finally closed at Somerton Park for the last time when they were expelled from the Vauxhall Conference in 1989. It was the end for a club who first started life in 1912 and made the first of 11 applications for re-election just three years later. Original members of Division Three in 1920 and Division Three South a year later, it was not until after the war that they plied their trade in a higher League. The first few years were a bit of a struggle, and they finished bottom in 1923 and again in 1934. In 1931 they finished second from bottom and were expelled from the League when they were thrown into financial turmoil. A bookmaker from Cardiff bought the ground for £7,000 and saved them on this occasion. They regained their League status in 1934 and lingered around the bottom of the table until 1938, when something miraculous happened. After finishing 16th the previous season, they won the League in 1939, but it was not until after the war that they played their first game in Division Two. By then, the promotion-winning team was long gone and they finished bottom and nine points away from safety, never to rise to such heights again.

They battled on through the 1940s and 1950s without ever really setting the world alight and were soon relegated to the newly formed Division Four in 1962. In 1969 they made the first of three successive applications for re-election, and each one was followed by financial crisis. Brian Eastwick, who was later to manage the club, once told the Press that Newport did not need a manager, they needed the world-famous escapologist Houdini. On each of the occasions that they applied for re-election they were saved by loans from businessmen, the city council and even the Welsh FA, who helped them to clear debts of £40,000. A couple of seasons before Tommy's arrival, Manchester United and Coventry came to Somerton Park to play benefit matches so they could pay off the inland revenue who were suing them for £14,000 in unpaid taxes. The end finally came in 1989, a year after they were temporarily saved yet again by an American businessman called Jerry Sherman, who came from Newport in Washington. His failure to pay ground rent meant that it was the end of the road for Newport County.

At the time Tommy joined the club, however, there was a new wave of optimism quietly coming in, as Andrew Taylor from the club explains:

'Len Ashurst arrived on the back of some miraculous work by Colin Addison. In the 1976–77 season, which will forever be known as the "Great Escape", we were within 48 hours of going out of business and way adrift at the bottom when "Addo" took over in the January. Manchester United played a fund-raising game for us, as did Coventry. The turnaround was nothing short of sensational and it all came down to the last two games of the season away and home to Workington. We won both games 1–0 to finish 19th and poor old Workington instead lost their League status and were replaced by Wimbledon. The following season we had a fair few injuries and were unsettled because "Addo" was constantly being linked with other clubs, and so we fell away to finish 16th. However, we just felt that things were about to turn for the better – but not in our wildest dreams did we realise just how much! Something was in the air though as we had 2,000 turn up for the Club Open Day in September!'

When Tommy signed in February, for a club record £25,000, County were nicely situated in eighth place and had enjoyed some rare giant-killing in the FA Cup, beating a West Ham team with the like of Trevor Brooking, Billy Bonds and Frank Lampard 2–1. In typical Newport fashion they lost after a replay in the next round to Colchester knowing that a visit from Manchester United was the prize awaiting the winner in the next round! However, this had brought much needed revenue and a sense of belief that undoubtedly spurred the club in to its future success. Dave Bruton had also added experience to the side and two brilliant local youngsters and future Welsh internationals, Steve Lowndes and Nigel Vaughan, had also broken through. Around the same time Tommy put pen to paper, winger Kevin Moore was signed from Swansea and the jigsaw was almost complete. It just needed Tommy to start firing on all cylinders!

It is not unfair to say that it took Tommy a little while to settle in at Newport. It was a long way down south and for the first few months he was away from Elaine in Sheffield and miles from his beloved Liverpool. Despite the fact that he was happy to be away from Lincoln, Wales still felt like a foreign place to Tommy.

However, disillusioned from his time at Sincil Bank, he knew that this could be his last chance of playing professional football – if he failed at Newport then there was nowhere else to go! He simply had to put his faith in his former manager Len Ashurst to get him back on track – and didn't he just! In his wildest dreams Tommy could not have predicted what was in store for him and the little Welsh Club over the next few seasons.

And yet the optimism sweeping through Somerton Park was not fully appreciated by Tommy. He was far more self-consumed with his own worries at that time and admitted that he made his move for one man. Tommy explains:

'I never came to Newport for County – I came for Len. He told me that he'd been approached by other managers wanting the lowdown on me and had put them off by saying I was trouble,

while at the same time he worked on his board to break the club transfer record for the third time that season! He told me Newport wasn't the best of places but that is was a lovely club and that people there couldn't do enough for you. He was so right! I was about half a stone overweight and had some money worries, and to be truthful Len rescued me. He told me to settle down in Newport and gave me a massive kick up the backside. That was something I got used to with Len over the years – he used to do it to keep me on my toes! He was a massive influence on me as was his assistant Jimmy Goodfellow.'

There was a good atmosphere in and around Somerton Park and Tommy soon felt part of the crowd. A number of the players were from the north-west and that helped him settle, but then again the locals were every bit as welcoming as Ashurst had promised. It could be said that he joined the club at the right time, the hunger for success was strong and he was just the catalyst they needed.

It was six months before Elaine was able to follow him south and set up home with Tommy, so apart from Len Ashurst and Jimmy Goodfellow he knew very few people. When he moved to Somerton Park he shared lodgings with a young midfielder called Neil Bailey and they soon became friends. Bailey went on to coach at the Manchester United School of Excellence which produced such players as Ryan Giggs, Paul Scholes, the Neville brothers and David Beckham. The club had a family atmosphere and he soon made friends with people from all over Wales, and when the goals started to flow with tremendous regularity he became their hero!

Tommy made his debut in a deserved 1–0 win at Huddersfield, who eventually ended the season below them in ninth place, and he made his home debut against Bradford City the following Tuesday, and although the Ironsides were beaten 4–2 he got his first goal on a mud heap of a pitch, justifying Ashurst's pre-match words to the Press:

'In Tynan's case he has to carry the tag of being Newport County's record signing, though this will not worry him – he has done a good job for me in the past and I have no doubt that he will do so again.'

Ashurst was pleased, although he recognised that Tommy was far from match fit and added after the game:

'Tommy hadn't played in any kind of competitive match from the week after Christmas until his debut at Huddersfield. As I've said before he is a penalty area player and the type of chance he took last Tuesday is the sort of goal he is always likely to get.'

This was followed by another goal in his third match against Doncaster. After a draw and defeats against Wimbledon and Barnsley, he scored the only goal against Crewe and another two points were in the bag. Newport went on to win the next four League games and Tommy added to his tally of goals against York and Aldershot. They were finally stopped at Darlington in a scrappy 1–0 defeat, but Tommy had already played 11 League matches and found the back of the net on five occasions. Perhaps, if it had been possible to move straight to Newport from Sheffield Wednesday without wasting a part of the season at Lincoln, his goals may have propelled Newport into the top four.

In his 115th League match Tommy scored one of the goals in a thrilling 3–2 win at Aldershot. A bit of a barren spell then followed, and he did not find the back of the net for another seven games. Despite the blip at Darlington, Newport's amazing form continued and they won another four consecutive League matches against Hereford, Torquay, Portsmouth and Scunthorpe. He finally broke his bad form at Port Vale, scoring Newport's goal in a 1–1 draw. County's form then wavered a little and Tommy finished the season playing in two victories and scoring a goal against Bournemouth. By the end of the season he had been involved in 20 matches for Newport and scored eight goals. With the team's decent form, there was a real buzz in the air at Somerton Park. Results had improved throughout the second half of the season and maybe the fans could sense that success was just around the corner.

However, the season's statistics suggest that Tommy was not yet firing on all cylinders. Andrew Taylor recalls:

> *'To be truthful Tommy was not really capturing the supporters' imagination. I have no doubt the pressure of the transfer fee didn't bother him – it was more about catching up on his match sharpness – but the fee was probably a greater concern for the fans who naturally expected a bit too much. Tommy himself has admitted that first season was not one of his better ones. We finished in eigth place, unable to make up the ground we had lost earlier in the season. It was the following year that we will always know as the "Season of Triumph" and was the one which made Tommy a cult hero.'*

In the summer Ashurst turned down the chance to return to Sunderland as manager, a decision that, without question, made an enormous difference to Tommy's future – and to that of a fellow Liverpudlian and future Anfield legend! Ashurst's brother, Robin, tipped the club to look at his work colleague at British Leyland, a forward plying his trade for South Liverpool. All it took was a fee of £3,500 and a bit of support to cure him of homesickness to transform the 21-year-old player and set him on his path to a career which would see him score more career goals than any other player since the war. And that young player's name was, of course, John Aldridge. Born in Liverpool on 18 September 1958, he signed for Newport on 2 May 1979 and eventually went on to be voted one of Liverpool's greatest players, an impressive achievement when you consider all of the world-class players who have donned the famous red shirt over the years.

By the time Newport sold him to Third Division Oxford United for £78,000 in March 1984, he had played 213 games for the club and scored 88 goals. He joined Oxford just in time to help them gain promotion from Division Three, as they began their greatest ever period in their footballing history, backed financially by controversial media tycoon Robert Maxwell. Aldridge's Oxford form saw him grab the attention of the club he idolised, Liverpool, and a £750,000 fee took him to Anfield. When he signed for Liverpool in 1987 he had smashed all sorts of records at Oxford, scoring 91 goals from 141 games.

During his relatively short stay at Liverpool (two and a half years) Aldridge was a key player in the Championship-winning team as well as being an FA Cup winner. When he left, towards the end of 1989, he had played 104 games for the Reds and scored 63 goals. He later became the first non-Basque player to represent Spanish side Real Sociedad when he moved there for £1 million, and he notched up 33 goals from 63 games. At the age of 33 he returned home to Liverpool to play for Second Division Tranmere Rovers for a transfer fee of £250,000 and made his debut on 17 August 1991. It was a fantastic bit of business for the Prenton Park club, who had aspirations of playing in the top flight, but, sadly, this was not to be. When he retired from playing in 1998 at the age of 38 he had scored a staggering 138 goals from 242 games for Rovers. He became player-manager of Rovers in 1996 and he continued as manager for a few seasons after his playing career had ended without much success. Aldridge managed a career total of 672 games and 362 goals, a post-war record at the time. On John Aldridge, Tommy has gone on record saying:

'"Aldo" worked hard and he took his chances to get to the very top of the game. And good luck to the bloke, even when he was famous he never changed. I remember Len once told me, "this lad will be the best foil you ever have because he has pace." I think he was right.'

In the summer of 1979, Tommy finally moved out of lodgings and into the club flat. Now that he had settled in the area, he wanted his own place and somewhere for his girlfriend to stay. By the end of the year Elaine would be with him, leaving Sheffield behind. When Tommy first arrived at the flat he was quite shocked by its condition but there were no major problems, all it needed was a few minor repairs, a lick of paint and some new carpets. The chairman was very supportive and offered to pay for the refurbishment. Tommy bought the carpets and décor and before long the place was looking really good, and it only cost him a fiver a week in rent. Out on the pitch, and with a few new players on board, pre-season had a positive feel to it and everyone hoped the team could make something happen. If everything gelled together and they got lucky, Tommy felt they had a real chance of pushing for promotion. With such a sense of optimism in and around the side, they were halfway there, and all they needed to do now was score more goals than they conceded during matches!

Despite the optimism, Newport's start to the 1979–80 season was a little up and down. It began well enough with with a 2–1 home win against Port vale and a 1–0 win at Aldershot, but these were followed by some inconsistent results. The one highlight was the introduction of Aldridge, although the 'star man' at Newport, striker Howard Goddard, broke his leg at Portsmouth, tragically scuppering his imminent move to First Division Portsmouth. By December Tommy had scored only seven, a disappointing tally by his own high expectations, and Len Ashurst went to the board and broke the record again with the £40,000 signing of veteran centre-forward Dave Gwyther. Gwyther was not an immediate threat to Tommy's place in the starting 11 as he injured himself soon after he arrived and missed a number of games, but when he was finally fit for action, Tommy's place was under a real threat because Aldridge had netted nine goals and was in too rich a vein of form to be dropped. It was not that Tommy had not shown glimpses of his capabilities, however. He was in outstanding form at home against Portsmouth on 6 November, when over 7,000 fans saw him net a brace in a thrilling 4–3 win at Fratton Park. Pompey had clawed their way back into the game three times, but Tommy finished them off with a spectacular headed winner from a John Relish free-kick.

Tommy was involved in a couple of big wins for Newport, beating Stockport 5–0 away and then Darlington 4–0 at home. After a goalless draw at Hartlepool they beat Scunthorpe 2–1 as the year came to an end, and as the Christmas lights came on in Newport town centre, people were suddenly beginning to think beyond the Fourth Division. County were showing signs they could become a promotion-winning team.

On 21 December, in the freezing cold, Tommy gave himself (and the fans) an early Christmas present when he scored the equaliser in a 1–1 draw at home to Peterborough, taking his tally for the season to seven.

Come January, however, both Tommy and Aldridge were going through a lean spell – but fortunately County's promotion rivals were dropping points and so they were holding onto a decent position in fourth spot. Dave Bruton's young brother Mick was signed and impressing in the reserves and briefly threatened for a first-team slot up front, and after three defeats in the previous four games, Tommy was left out for the game against Huddersfield. Things were not looking so good for Tommy, and Andrew Taylor picks up the story.

'You could see that Tommy was losing belief. Bruton was a big lad but looked short of it at that level and taking Tommy's place could not have helped his confidence; especially knowing that Gwyther was a quality player who would be in the side for sure when fit. And then it all began to change for Tommy – just as some supporters were beginning to write him off. Newport played Cardiff – always an occasion for us – in a Welsh Cup tie. We hadn't beaten

the Bluebirds in a competitive game in over 40 years and had a fairly young side out on the pitch with Tommy on the bench. Aldridge put us 1–0 up and Tommy came on not long after and was an absolute revelation! He wrapped it up with a header from a Walden cross seconds before the end and there was pandemonium in the stands! That night I really did feel that things were about to take off for us, and I somehow felt that Tommy was about to be all we had hoped when he had first signed.'

County were drawn away to another Second Division side in the next round, but League form was the worry – had they left it too late with 15 games left? In a home game against Doncaster, County again struggled and Ashurst brought on Tommy as an extra attacker in place of defender Grant Davies. Tommy again made an impact, and with the final whistle approaching, County having equalised through Aldridge, Tommy sent through Steve Lowndes to score the winner with seconds remaining. Wrexham then went the same way as Cardiff and in the following games Tommy continued his role as a super sub match saviour as County chalked up 12 successive victories, including a Welsh Cup semi-final win over Merthyr. Tommy scored with a cracking header in a 2–0 win. Ahead of them, in the two-leg Final, was Shrewsbury Town, and the winner won a place in Europe.

By Easter the fans really believed that at long last this could be County's season. On the Bank Holiday Monday at Hereford County they won 1–0 with a huge away contingent cheering them on. Kevin Moore was sent off, however, which put him out for the game the next day at Peterborough. With other knocks and niggles affecting the squad, Ashurst changed tactics and played Tommy in midfield in a 4–4–2 system. It worked and another 1–0 win was in the bag!

While this run of form was focusing the minds of the squad, things got even better without even a ball being kicked by Newport! Swansea met Shrewsbury in the other Welsh Cup semi-final, and in dramatic fashion future County record signing and ex-Liverpool forward Alan Waddle missed for the Swans in a penalty shoot-out. Shrewsbury qualified for the Final against Newport, but as they were an English side 'guesting' in the competition they were not eligible for European qualification if they won, which meant that County would be in Europe by default no matter what the result. It was definitely celebration time for County!

Come the last two games of the season promotion was all but in County's hands. Indeed, the penultimate game at lowly Rochdale looked a certainty to bring out the champagne. County just needed to win – and failure to do so was unthinkable, as it would mean a win would be needed at Championship-chasing Walsall in the final game. Sure enough, County lost 2–0 and needed the result against Walsall!

Coach after coach made the journey from Wales to Walsall and all resonated to what by then had become the most popular anthem with all County's followers: 'One Tommy Tynan, there's only one Tommy Tynan!' Tommy had regained his place in the starting line up and was not about to let this chance to put his name in the record books slip out of his grasp. County won 4–2 in emotional scenes and Tommy scored the all-decisive fourth which put a fightback out of reach for Walsall and sent County up in third place. Tommy himself sums up that season:

'I did have a difficult spell which wasn't nice and I even went on the transfer list. I went to Len and he said he had a problem in the midfield and asked me if I fancied it. I ended up doing quite well and scoring a few, mainly coming on as sub. It suited me getting into the box late from a midfield position. A club came in for me but I turned it down as I really felt we could do it – and the crowd were getting behind me.

Although Walsall were playing for the Championship I felt we were the better side. There was a lot of apprehension but I felt we would do it.'

That still left the Welsh Cup to play for over two legs. Just three days after clinching that long awaited promotion at Walsall, Tommy and his teammates and several thousand, still hung over, County followers arrived at Somerton Park in party mood. Cup fever had gripped the Newport area.

The first Welsh Cup was won by Wrexham back in 1877 when they beat the Druids 1–0, and they have gone on to lift the trophy a record 23 times to date. Cardiff City have been winners on 22 occasions and Swansea have won it 10 times. Newport had made it to the Final before but they had never won it.

The night was not as tense as perhaps it could have been, given that qualification to the European Cup-Winners' Cup had already been secured. Nevertheless, this was only County's second appearance in the Final of a competition that had, with the exception of the two World Wars, been fiercely contested every year since 1877. In 1963 County had been mortally embarrassed, on a 2–1 aggregate, by village side Borough United. Their opponents now – despite being on the wrong side of the border – were the existing holders and had taken the splendid trophy back to Gay Meadow on four occasions since they first lifted it in 1891. Indeed, Shrewsbury had enjoyed a successful season in an extremely competitive Second Division campaign, which had seen them do the 'double' over Chelsea, claim the scalps of the likes of Newcastle and QPR, and just 10 days previously win 3–1 at West Ham before thumping Fulham 5–2 in their final League game. Their manager, Graham Turner, was in no mood to relinquish the silverware gracing the boardroom of their picturesque ground and surrender to a team two Divisions below – promotion winners or not!

Tommy stood, arms folded, between goalkeeper Gary Plumley and his ultra consistent former Sheffield Wednesday teammate Richard Walden for the historic pre-match team photo, and all of the County fans in the season's best attendance of 9,950 hoped that this would be another iconic moment as he cemented his legendary status in that part of Wales.

Still revelling in his new deep-lying role which had seen him contribute so many important goals in the season run-in, Tommy gave a Man of the Match performance which was heralded with an early goal as he stretched to slot home from the edge of the six yard box in typical predatory fashion after Aldridge had nodded down a cross from Walden. A scrambled equalizer, just before half-time, looked to make a game of it, but there was no suppressing Tommy, who, with minutes ticking to the final whistle, scored the winner with a low shot from the edge of the area. Pandemonium broke out, and a short while later thousands were on the pitch demanding that their players reappear to take a bow. A special cheer was reserved for their two-goal hero.

After the second leg, two days and 90 minutes later, a blood spattered Tommy lifted the Cup in front of an adoring Newport public. County had given a master class and Tommy was imperious. Countless cars and 37 coaches had made the journey and witnessed a game that Tommy counts among his most memorable. Just 12 minutes in Tommy opened the scoring with Aldridge again the supplier, and the only scare came from a missed penalty before Steve Lowndes added a second to put the game beyond reach before half-time. Fourteen minutes from time County made it the Shrews' heaviest home defeat of the season. Tommy sent Aldridge away on the right flank and superb footwork from big Dave Gwyther sent the huge County following delirious. County had beaten three Second Division sides on their way to their so long awaited first major piece of silverware.

Tommy enjoyed the occasion even more than the promotion decider:

'What was so special was the fans' reaction. I walked into the bar after the game and was given a few bottles of champagne – a pity

I don't like the stuff! Success breeds success and it changed everyone's perspective about the club. It was one of the best nights ever. I remember vividly walking through town the next day and it was unbelievable. To be honest it was even better than after the Carl Zeiss Jena game for me.'

The people of Newport turned out in their thousands on the 21st to see Tommy and the team parade the Cup on an open-top bus tour through the town as they visited the Civic Centre for a reception with the mayor. County had achieved nothing of note since 1939 and now, in the space of weeks, had won promotion, the Welsh Cup and had qualified for Europe! Little could Tommy have known just how much that adventure would put the media spotlight on him during the next season.

Chapter 12
The European Cup-Winners' Cup

Tommy's second full season at Newport County proved to be one of the most memorable of his career due largely to his exploits in Europe. Len Ashurst's team were no longer languishing in the basement division and after the triumphs of the previous season, and a few new signings, most supporters were hoping they could consolidate their position and avoid a relegation struggle. With teams like Fulham, Charlton Athletic, Sheffield United and Huddersfield Town to face, it was not going to be easy. With the added bonus of European football, Somerton Park could look forward to some large crowds and intense media coverage, as well as earning themselves a few quid in the process. Considered the third most important European trophy, the Cup-Winners' Cup came into existence in 1960 when Fiorentina of Italy lifted it. The last team to win it were Lazio, who beat Real Mallorca on 19 May 1999 at Villa Park. During its 39-year existence, British teams Tottenham Hotspur, West Ham United, Manchester City, Chelsea, Rangers, Aberdeen, Everton, Manchester United and Arsenal all won the trophy. Chelsea won two Cup-winners' Cups along with AC Milan and Dynamo Kiev, but the record number of wins goes to Barcelona, who lifted the trophy on four occasions. Qualification for the competition came by winning a major domestic trophy, and many top clubs have cast envious eyes at the likes of Cardiff and Wrexham competing on the European stage thanks to them winning their domestic Cup competition. Although the Cup was somewhat devalued in its latter years by the Champions League, it is a competition which holds fantastic memories for the millions of fans who have been to a Cup-Winners' Cup match.

Newport opened the 1980–81 season at Turf Moor against Burnley, who had been relegated from the Second Division the previous season along with Fulham and Charlton. They were pleased to come away with a point after a 1–1 draw and followed this with a narrow defeat at home against Charlton Athletic, who beat them 2–1, with Tommy getting what turned out to be a consolation goal. He followed that up with both goals in a 2–1 home win over Millwall.

It is worth noting that Len Ashurst was still using Tommy as a midfielder most of the time, preferring Dave Gwyther and John Aldridge as the two centre-forwards.

Goals were hard to come by and Tommy only added a further two before Christmas. It was not until the last third of the season that Tommy established a permanent partnership up front with Gwyther, and this time Aldridge was the player to lose his place. And what a difference it made. After that, there was no turning back and Tommy finished the season with 20 goals and as Player of the Year. County finished in a more than respectable 12th position but without doubt their focus on the League had been difficult to maintain in the light of the excitement of their European adventure.

Tommy's 25th birthday came and went, and results were still up and down into the new year. Away from the pitch, though, Tommy experienced happy times when his daughter, Jordanna, came into the world on 15 December 1980. As much as he was enjoying time with his daughter, back on the pitch he was unhappy as he was still not playing up front. His ability with the ball and the way he could come through defenders provided attacking options from midfield, but he was not able to put it into the back of the net like he could if he was playing at centre-forward. He may well have added another 10 or 15 goals to his end-of-season total of 20 from 55 if he had been playing up front all season, although 20 goals was a more than respectable tally for a centre-forward, let alone a midfielder. However, the number of goals he scored in midfield coupled with the number he created for those playing up front could fully justify Len Ashurst's decision. Len had the best of both worlds – he had record signing Dave Gwyther up front, with John Aldridge and Tommy doing the business in the middle of the park bringing the ball through.

Once Tommy was restored to his favoured role as a centre-forward alongside Gwyther, he decided to make sure that managers in the future would find it impossible to play him anywhere else.

Rotherham, Chester and Charlton were promoted that season, with Hull, Blackpool, Colchester and Sheffield United falling through the trapdoor into the Fourth Division. Southend, Lincoln, Doncaster and Wimbledon, who would be competing in the top flight five years later, replaced them and both Bristol sides were relegated from Division Two along with Preston. The job was done as Newport had achieved mid-table respectability, but this was not why everyone was talking about the little Welsh club that season.

Newport County started their Cup-Winners' Cup adventure by thrashing Northern Irish side Crusaders 4–0 at a packed Somerton Park. Despite the advantage, they feared the return leg, which was due to be played in Belfast. Amid bombings, shootings and hunger strikes, Newport were going to the province at one of the bloodiest times in its history. As the coach drove through the city, Tommy saw the devastation for himself as they passed burnt-out houses and cars. The streets were awash with soldiers, and murals were displayed on the walls of houses and parks. He recalls that there must have been a local election going on at the time because he saw a huge sign on one of the walls that read 'Vote for Tynan'.

On a pre-season tour of Ireland a few years later, Tommy found out that the origins of his surname were indeed Irish. He was in a pub and the bar manager came up to him and asked if he was Tommy Tynan. Being so far from home Tommy was shocked that anyone recognised him:

> *'Here we were, an English team in deepest darkest Northern Ireland, right at the height of the troubles, and I noticed this big paddy landlord looking at me from behind the bar. It was a bit unnerving, I can tell you now, and I wasn't sure if he was gonna pull out a shooter and blow me away or what the hell he was up to! Fortunately, he had been following Newport's Cup run in the paper and he recognised me from a picture he had seen. When we knew we were all friends, he poured me a drink and took me out the back of the pub where he asked me for an autograph and then he showed me some big old family book. Inside was the name Tynan and there was a bit on the history and origins of the name. Apparently, it's very popular down Kilkenny way, and there's even an abbey named after me! He also told me that there was once an Irish hurling team and all the players were called Tynan, which must have been murder for the commentators. I don't know if he was pulling my leg or if he had been sampling too much of what he was selling behind the bar!'*

Tommy's Irish roots can be traced back to his mother's parents. Tommy has no memory of his grandfather, but he can recall that his Granny Murphy was quite well spoken and that she died from shock when she was in her 90s. She was skipping out in the street with the children and landed awkwardly and broke her ankles.

Belfast had a devastated, uneasy feel and it cast a shadow over the streets as they made their way to the ground. It felt like the whole place had been left to its own devices. It did not matter which side of the divide you were living on, the sense of loss and the funeral marches were never-ending. In the middle of this, the citizens of Northern Ireland continued with what they called normal life.

Fortunately, Newport County were not sufficiently disturbed by the atmosphere, and in a hard-fought encounter they gave a good account of themselves. The Crusaders gave it a go but ultimately provided little threat and the match ended goalless. The fans went back to Wales delighted at the prospect of being in the hat for the second round of the Cup. Despite the concerns, Tommy has extremely fond memories of the trip:

> *'My abiding memory is the hospitality they gave us – it was second to none. Their players were waiting for us as we came out after the game to look after each of us on a one-to-one basis and they bought us all a Guinness. We found out the next day though that their secretary had been robbed at gunpoint after the game!'*

They had mixed feelings about being drawn against Norwegian side Haugar Hsugesund, but these fears were short-lived. They drew 0–0 in Norway before hammering them 6–0 at home, and Tommy scored a couple of screamers in the process.

> *'I was a sub in Haugar – it was freezing! Of all the goals I scored, the one in the second leg is the one of which I am most proud. One of the major football magazines – either* Shoot *or* Match Weekly *– did a feature about it saying how well I'd done to come out of the hole to play the ball out to the wing and then get back into the box to score. That one was very satisfying.'*

Newport had been paired with East German side Carl Zeiss Jena for the quarter-final, who were one of the top sides in Germany throughout the 1960s and 1970s. Founded in 1903 by workers from the nearby Carl Zeiss optics factory, after various name changes they established themselves as a top-flight team under Hitler's Third Reich. Nazi reorganisation of football saw them in among the elite, and they won the League in 1935, 1936, 1940 and 1941. Playing at the Ernst Abbe Sportfeld, they later established themselves as a top East German side and won the League three times and the Cup on four occasions by the time Newport County arrived in Germany for the first leg. Carl Zeiss had beaten AS Roma and Valencia in previous rounds but they were not prepared for the blood and guts tiny Newport County showed that night. The Welsh wizards matched the Germans and stood toe-to-toe with them for 90 minutes. For Tommy, it was one of the biggest games of his career as he scored both goals in the 2–2 draw. Suddenly, Tommy and the boys were big news and everyone wanted a piece of them. Tommy remembers the the way in which the Carl Zeiss Jena game catapulted the club into the media spotlight.

'We were expected to get slaughtered! Len and Jimmy let us have a few drinks in the hotel the night before the game, much to the amazement of the Germans. The Berlin Wall was still up at that time and it had taken us forever to get there through all the checkpoints, each one guarded by soldiers carrying machine guns! It was quite frightening and very humbling when we saw the lifestyle the locals had to put up with.

When you look up at the end of a game and see CZJ 2 – Newport 2 (Tynan 2), well it is of course one of the most memorable highlights of my career. The media frenzy afterwards was something else and gave us a taste of what the top stars go through – it was quite frightening actually!

The home game was the most nervous I've ever been and losing 1–0 when we absolutely battered them from start to finish was the biggest disappointment of my career. I was still getting a load of media attention, however, so Len did what he felt he had to every now and again to get me out of the limelight – and dropped me!'

It seems a pattern emerges when we look back over Newport's history, that any little glimmer of success is rapidly followed by bad luck, and in the return leg they were haunted yet again. In front of 18,000 at Somerton Park, Newport County were just minutes away from a Cup-Winners' Cup semi-final encounter with Benfica. The East Germans narrowly beat Newport 1–0 in the second leg and suddenly it was all over. They had done everything but hit the back of the net that night, with shots, headers and countless chances hitting the crossbar, hitting the post and being cleared off the line. It had been an adventure of a lifetime for the Welshmen. Another Welsh Cup win could have seen them having another stab at Europe now they had developed a taste for the big occasion, but sadly this was never to be and Newport proved to be a one hit wonder in Europe as well as in the Welsh Cup. However, Tommy was on a high and he married Elaine on 17 July 1981 at the Mendey Methodist Church, and he chose his brother-in-law, Brian Rivetts, to be his best man. On the pitch he had formed a formidable striking partnership with John Aldridge, and although Tommy was aware that Aldridge was something special, he knew he was by no means the finished article at Newport. It took him a little while to build the physique, which gave him such pace and sublime finishing. Tommy believes that it was under Jim Smith at Oxford United that Aldridge started to show the first signs of being a world-class footballer.

However, for Newport a struggle lay ahead, and by the end of the decade they would no longer exist.

Chapter 13
Good Old County

Duxring the summer of 1981 Shergar won the Derby by a clear 10 lengths, and on 22 May Mark Chapman pleaded guilty to the murder of John Lennon and was sentenced to life in prison. The summer of 1981 was also the year cricketer Ian Botham quit England. Back at Newport, and with extra money in the coffers from the two Cup runs, Len Ashurst was planning to spend. All he had to do now was convince the board. It was this that would ultimately lead to his downfall.

To get the money, he had to make an impossible promise. He told the board if they gave him the money he would get them promoted. With their heads still full of visions of the big time, they agreed to let him spend as they dreamed of Anfield and Old Trafford, when they should have been thinking about Roots Hall and Ashton Gate, the first two places they would visit that season in the League. Len had put his head on the block and in the end he was not around to see the end of the season, but he certainly spent big before he left. He signed Alan Waddle for £80,000, at a time when £80,000 was an extremely large amount of money for a side the size of Newport. Waddle had been at Liverpool with Tommy and had played in the first team, scoring in a Merseyside derby, but despite this, Tommy did not really rate him at the top level, although he was sure he would prove effective at this level. Len also bought Jeff Johnson for £60,000 and both players were on triple the wages of the rest of the squad. Financial problems resurfaced, and amid all the European football and fancy newspaper articles Newport soon discovered that they were living beyond their means. With an average attendance of 3,000–4,000, now that the Cup fever was over, they still had bills to pay.

Despite Tommy opening the 1981–82 League campaign with a lovely goal in a 4–0 win against Southend, Newport's League form was just as unpredictable as it had been the previous season. In the next four games Tommy was involved in, they picked up just two points and were beaten at home by Brentford. Oldham Athletic knocked them out of the League Cup in the second round and Tommy scored his next goals during his 210th League game as they drew 2–2 against former club Lincoln City up at their place. Results did not improve until Newport beat Wimbledon 3–2 at Plough Lane and Tommy scored again. By now he had been involved in 13 League matches that season and they had only won three. The pressure was really on Len, and the gates were sinking ever lower. Instead of mixing it at the top of the League with the big boys, they found themselves at the wrong end of the table. Instead of dreaming about getting their money back and moving into a higher League, the board were heading towards a financial crisis at full speed. After the Wimbledon game, Tommy had to wait for another six matches until his next goal and it was against an up-and-coming Oxford United team. After this he was involved in another eight League victories for Newport and bagged a further seven goals. Most of these wins were at home but at least they helped keep them in the division. There was not even a decent Cup run to enjoy – they were knocked out in the first round of the FA Cup by Fourth Division Colchester United and followed this up with some pretty dire performances in the League. Luckily, in Tynan and Aldridge Newport had enough quality to avoid the drop that season and they kept ticking along for a little while longer. They even had one more try at promotion the following season before everything began to disintegrate and their star players were sold. County were finally relegated in 1987 never to return; by which time both John Aldridge and Tommy had left the club.

Len's spending really did signal the beginning of the end for the club, and for himself, as they lurched into their final financial crisis. Although they would reform as Newport AFC a little while later, they had lost their beloved Somerton Park as the developers moved in. Len's gamble did not pay off and he was sacked before the end of the season. Colin Addison rejoined and after a shaky start managed to steer the club to safety in the penultimate game. But an incident in the final match at home to Swindon put the fear of God into Tommy!

> *'I did a stupid thing in the game against Swindon and have regretted it ever since. I took a penalty knowing it would probably relegate them – it was in front of their fans and as I prepared to take it they started knocking down the billboards. I scored and gave them a thumbs down, which was out of order really, and they broke through to get at me! It was pretty scary!'*

The statistics for the season read: played 46, won 14, lost 16 and drawn 16. They finished with 58 points, and Tommy scored 13 goals. In March 1982 Len Ashurst moved on to Carlisle United, then Cardiff City, where he tried unsuccessfully to sign Tommy for a third time. He also spent a season as the manager of his beloved Sunderland, the team he made his League debut for in 1957 as an 18-year-old full-back.

At the end of the season in the top flight, Liverpool wrestled the League title back from Aston Villa, who were rather preoccupied with winning the European Cup and finished a lowly 11th. And what of Tommy's other teams? Swansea City faired best, finishing sixth just two points behind Arsenal in Division One. Sheffield Wednesday just missed out on promotion to the top flight as they finished fourth in Division Two and Rotherham United, who he was due to join in a short while, finished three places behind them. Lincoln City just missed out on promotion from Division Three and, in the same

League, it was another season of underachievement for Plymouth Argyle as they finished in 10th position with 65 points.

Other notable events happening in the latter part of 1981 included the closures at British Leyland which were announced in October and resulted in the loss of nearly 300 jobs. On 18 November England beat Hungary 1–0 at Wembley and qualified for the 1982 World Cup in Spain. This gave UK garages something else to flog as all sorts of bandwagons started rolling and Spain '82 merchandise was purchased en masse, in the hope our boys would lift the trophy once again.

In his last season for Newport County Tommy was on fire and it marked the beginning of an era when he became one of the most predatory centre-forwards ever to grace the lower Leagues. Gone were the days of playing around in midfield. It is true to say that Tommy scored a lot of goals from midfield, but he had proven that he could score even more if he was given the chance to play in his natural position at Liverpool, where he regularly finished top scorer for the reserves as well as the A and B teams. At Sheffield Wednesday he also scored a number of goals from midfield, and was even voted Player of the Year, but he was still most effective in a centre-forward pairing. He had the kind of instinctive ability that made him a natural goalscorer and it was those skills that gave him a sense of freedom and which often led him into the right position to receive the ball and put it in the back of the net.

There have been stories related to me during the research of this book about how seriously Tommy took training and how he wanted to score on every occasion, whether in a practice match or a vital Cup game, and between the years 1980 and 1990 he scored 226 goals from 503 matches.

Tommy had finally arrived, and he scored 124 goals in the next five seasons just to prove it. There was also controversy ahead for him but those were not the only headlines he would make. A few years later people would be calling him many great names, such as 'legend' and 'cult hero'.

When I arrived on the terraces of Plymouth Argyle under my dad's coat a few years later, I was one of the thousands of youngsters who were in awe of his skill and tried to copy it in the playground. Defenders feared the man as his goals took Newport to the brink that year. The cracks were, however, too large to ignore now. For a while it had looked as if good things were going to happen at the Welsh club when Colin Addison had taken the reins, but nobody would have guessed they would miss out on promotion and that the very worst would eventually happen.

And so, the 1982–83 season began.

Newport started their League campaign with a draw away to Doncaster Rovers. Tommy scored the only goal in a win against Chesterfield, before they drew at home to Plymouth Argyle once again. A couple of wins against Huddersfield and Portsmouth were followed by a defeat, then three more wins. Tommy hit one in the first win against Lincoln and another against Bristol Rovers, before scoring two more in a 5–1 win up at Orient. From his first 10 League games Tommy had scored seven goals and it did not stop there. There was another as they took the scalp of Sheffield United and then one more against Reading. As the mid-point of the season arrived, Newport were promotion contenders and the goals kept coming. While the mind-numbing PA system blared out the hits of 1983, such as *You Can't Hurry Love* and *Billie Jean,* optimistic Welshmen sipped weak tea on the terraces, filled with a sense of false optimism. Tommy was on the winning side seven times in a row as they beat the likes of Wigan Athletic, Oxford United and rivals Cardiff City. If they could just keep up the pace promotion was in the bag. Andrew Taylor takes up the story of the season:

'Because we had only just stayed up and only briefly dabbled in the transfer market, bringing in Kenny Stroud and Vaughan Jones, we didn't really expect too much from that season. As it happens, we played some of the best football ever seen at Somerton Park – a really

attractive, expansive game – and Tommy became the consistent goal machine we had always hoped for. He scored 33 that season, and with Aldridge getting 20 and Lowndes 15, we were a joy to behold! We enjoyed four fantastic games against Everton in both Cup competitions, drawing two of them, and at Easter after beating Cardiff (how I love saying that!) we looked as though no one could catch us. We needed something like seven points from our last seven games to get promoted – and managed to win just the once – beating Wrexham 4-0 with Tommy getting a hat-trick. I have asked Tommy what went wrong. In fact I have asked just about everybody involved with the side that season and no one can be sure. Some suggest that they were over trained, others that the pressure just got too much. The more fanciful even suggest that they didn't want to go up! What is for sure is that it was the beginning of the end. That side broke up at the end of the season, with Tommy moving on to Plymouth for an unforgivably low fee of £55,000 and things were nowhere near the same again. It could and should have been all so different!'

Tommy adds,

'We died a death! I don't think we realised the position we were in. Bottling it is a bad expression for me to use…but…'

Newport went out in the second round of the League Cup once again. They did, however, give high-flying Everton a run for their money, but eventually lost 4–2. In the second leg they went to Goodison Park and pulled off a 2–2 draw, with Tommy letting fly once again. They later drew them again in the third round of the FA Cup and held them once more. This time, at Somerton Park, they drew 1–1 with the Toffeemen. Defeating Enfield and Orient along the way, they were set for another showdown at Goodison, but were narrowly beaten 2–1 after giving it their all. Manchester United went on to win the trophy that year, beating Brighton & Hove Albion at Wembley, but Newport put on a good show against Everton, who were one of the best sides in the top flight at the time, so it was not all bad news. Tommy played in nine League and FA Cup games that season and chalked up six goals to add to his total of 33 from 59 games. Those figures do not include the five he scored in the Welsh Cup that year.

The Tynan–Aldridge partnership may have set the League alight that season, but it also came to a premature end. If the financial backing had been there, Newport could surely have climbed the Leagues. Wimbledon were on the way to the top flight, but it could just as easily have been Newport. Both clubs had similar set-ups, with Wimbledon playing at Plough Lane and coming from non-League origins. It seems sad that Newport, who battled against all the odds for survival and not success, were soon to come to the end of the line. The Tynan–Aldridge partnership ended because the club had to sell their best players to survive and Tommy was part of the exodus, ending up at Plymouth, quickly followed by the departure of Aldridge. Addison had spent the summer getting them all fit and they had blown it right at the death. Now players such as Steve Lowndes and Nigel Vaughan were on their way out of Somerton as they tried to balance the books.

At the time Tommy was not looking for a move. Yes, he was looking around to see whose ears had been pricked up by his 33 goals, but he was quite happy at Somerton Park. He had no notion that he would not be about for another stab at promotion until Colin Addison appeared on his doorstep one day. Tommy ushered Addison inside and, over a cup of coffee, he was told that the club really did not have any other option but to sell him because of their financial state. County needed around £200,000 to survive and he told Tommy that they were going to take the first reasonable offer for him if he agreed. That offer came from Plymouth Argyle, and their manager Bobby Moncur turned up at the office a couple of days later. The secretary led them into Colin Addison's office and Tommy was told that a fee had been agreed and all they needed to do was sort out his personal terms. Tommy was disappointed but pragmatic.

'I was very sad about it. I had a bond with people there and was so lucky that I managed to eventually forge that at Plymouth as well. The last time I drove past where the old ground was and saw houses there instead – it was one of the saddest things I've seen. To think I played in a European Cup quarter-final there! The place was wonderful.'

Moncur offered Tommy £300 a week and a £5,000 relocation fee, which was not a bad offer. In two minds, Tommy took up Moncur's offer to have a look at the city, having only ever seen Home Park and nothing more. It was during this visit, when he stayed at the Holiday Inn on Plymouth Hoe, that he decided to make the move. The two men had a meal in the executive suite before Moncur took him to his home on the edge of Yelverton golf course to meet his family. Tommy was highly impressed by Bobby Moncur. The only other manager to impress him as much was George Graham, who tried to sign him from Plymouth when he was manager at Millwall. The Lions paid for Tommy to go up to the capital to talk to George and the Scotsman pulled out all the stops that day. Money was the sticking point though as the wages Millwall were offering were the same as he was on at Plymouth, plus a 10 grand relocation fee, but the price of living in the capital was much higher.

Bobby Moncur's offer was very tempting, Tommy liked the feel of the city and there was certainly no future for him at Newport County. The Plymouth manager's charisma finally won through and Tommy Tynan signed for Plymouth Argyle on a two-year contract in August 1983 for a fee of £55,000.

Chapter 14
Up for the Cup

Plymouth Argyle came into existence in 1886. Teams like Aston Villa, West Bromwich Albion and the two Blackburn sides (Olympic and Rovers) were all winning the FA Cup and suddenly a number of new clubs were starting up and applying for League status. Meetings were taking place in pubs and clubs, discussions and rules were being laid down over a few pints and the institutions we now have today were being born. Argyle played in the Southern League at the turn of the century, with teams like Preston North End, Sunderland and Sheffield Wednesday the early pace-setters. Argyle FC played their first match against Dunheved College in Launceston and they lost 2–0. They followed this by beating Plymouth College 2–1 at the College Ground on the 30th, but they were still a good few years away from playing professionally. First club captain F.H. Grose and W. Pethybridge are credited with founding the club. They were at college in Launceston and travelled to Plymouth to play. The men had lodgings in Argyll Terrace, Plymouth, and this is partly how the club got its bizarre second name. Also, Grose and Pethybridge were keen followers of the Argyll and Sutherland regimental football team, who donned green shirts, so the regiment must have influenced the two men.

The following year, under new club president Clarence Spooner, a rule book was published and the foundations of today's game were set in place. At that time home games were being played at Marsh Mills, but Argyle's first few matches had been played at Mount Gould and specially chartered trains were laid on to take supporters along the water's edge towards the leafy canopies of Plymbridge Woods. The final foundations were laid when the club turned professional in 1903 and they acquired Home Park. The ground had been unused for three years after the original tenants Devonport Albion Rugby Club could not settle a dispute about rent with the landlords and Clarence Spooner obtained a lease. His Argyll Athletics Club moved in for the meet in Whitson in 1901 and Argyle FC began renting the place from the athletics club in 1903 for £300 a year. They had finally acquired a decent site to begin their life as a professional outfit. All they needed to do now was bring in a team manager with sufficient experience, and Irishman Frank Brettell, the former secretary of Everton and Bolton Wanderers, joined the Greens for the start of the 1903–04 Southern League campaign. They finished the season in ninth position and over 15,000 people came to see a match against Newcastle United. The gate for the Aston Villa match the following year was even more impressive, and at least 21,000 came to watch. After only one season Brettell quit as manager and Robert Jack took up the post in 1904. Jack stayed for just a year, then William Fullerton took over for a year and after that the club were without a manager for the next three seasons. It was quite a surprise when they came second in 1908, but after finishing 11th in 1910 they were nearly wound up and Jack was put back in charge to steady the ship, where he stayed until 1938. He was instrumental in getting Argyle elected to Division Three in 1920 and winning promotion to the second tier in 1930.

It was not always light and happiness at Home Park, however, and things were so bad in the beginning that Stanley and Clarence Spooner had to form a new board to save the club from financial ruin. Another man who helped shape and guide the club was Mr A.C. Ballard, a local businessman and a chairman of the club. Described as a man ahead of his time, he offered to fly the team to away matches in 1933, and although he trialled the idea and beat the team to the ground by many hours, his offer was never taken up. Division Three began in 1920 and after one year it evolved into two separate North and South Leagues with one team from each gaining promotion to the second tier. Argyle finished as runners-up to Southampton at the end of that inaugural season. In fact, they finished second for six successive seasons behind the likes of Bristol City, Portsmouth, Swansea Town and Reading. They missed out by the narrowest of goal differences in 1922, they really were that unlucky.

When Robert Jack took them to the Second Division in 1930 they held their own in the higher League and had a good crack at promotion to the top flight in 1932 and again in 1937 before the war interrupted their efforts. Jack Tresadern managed the club throughout the war years and Jimmy Rae joined in 1947 and stayed for eight seasons. When the Football League programme resumed in 1946 Tresadern's team finished fourth from bottom and at the beginning of Rae's tenure things did not really improve. They milled about in the second tier for a few more years before relegation came in 1950. Two years later they regained their status as a Second Division club, but the 1950s were an up and down decade for the Pilgrims as they jumped between the two divisions before finishing fifth in the Second Division in 1962. This time they stayed there for eight years before relegation and they did not escape again until Billy Rafferty and Paul Mariner did the business in 1975.

It was a far from successful move for Tommy in the beginning. Plymouth was further away from Sheffield than Newport and this caused problems for his wife, whose family lived in the north. When they first arrived, Tommy, Elaine and the children stayed at a club-owned property at the entrance to Home Park which was run by former player George Robinson, who also looked after the apprentices. Tommy was amazed by the contrast, as Bobby Moncur had courted him with champagne and steak at one of Plymouth's luxury hotels and now they were living in a place that did not even have carpets:

> *'It was a bit of an anticlimax when coming from the Holiday Inn to the clubhouse, but it wasn't for long. When I came back on loan [for the promotion push in 1986] Leigh Cooper and his wife Karen put me up for a couple of months until I got myself sorted, so I would like to thank him for helping me to settle in so quickly.'*

During his time at the clubhouse Tommy was introduced to another local legend, the Cornish pasty, which were made for the apprentices and as big as the plate they came on. He and Elaine were the last people to stay at the clubhouse as shortly afterwards George Robinson and the apprentices moved out and it was sold three months later. By that time Tommy and Elaine had managed to sell their house in Newport. They then rented a house in the Mainstone area of Plymouth before moving to two other parts of the city during his first spell with the club. It was a big adjustment for Tommy and the beginning of his time at Argyle was one of the most barren periods of his professional career. This may have been, in part, due to the fact that he was unsettled off the pitch:

> *'We never really settled during my first spell at Argyle. We were so far away from the family it was difficult, especially for Elaine and the kids. When I came back from Rotherham, when I actually signed, we made our minds up that we were going to make a serious go of it in Plymouth, and we did. We made loads of friends and started to enjoy it.'*

Tommy's first competitive match in the green, black and white of Plymouth Argyle occured on 27 August 1983 in front of a home crowd of just 3,730. He made his debut against Wigan Athletic, who were at that time one of the new boys to the professional Leagues. The match ended without any goals and nobody set the world on fire, but Tommy was simply relieved to have completed his first match unscathed in front of the home fans.

> *'I was nervous, of course I was, and everything was new. I had to try to adapt to a new manager, new teammates and a different approach. It was tough in the beginning and I think the fact that the family hadn't settled did affect my game for a while.'*

Argyle followed this performance with defeats away at Millwall and Rotherham, with Tommy involved in both. Gordon Nisbet scored their first League goal of the season on 10 September and they drew 1–1 with Gillingham. Tommy's first League goal came the very next match against his old team, Lincoln City. Unfortunately, Argyle came away from Sincil Bank with nothing that day, losing 3–1, but Tommy felt an enormous sense of relief.

The first 15 games were a nightmare and the crowd were beginning to get on his back, but he was not about to give up. Never the easiest of fans, the Green Army have, over the years, been starved of success, and when goals did not come immediately the tide of optimism started to turn. The previous season had been half decent and the Pilgrims had finished eighth in the old Third Division. After relegation in 1977, and the loss of talismanic striker Paul Mariner, the side had plodded on without really making a decent attempt at promotion.

During the 1983–84 season, defeats were coming thick and fast for Argyle and attendances were down below the 4,000 mark as relegation looked imminent, although they gave a good account of themselves in the Cup against Arsenal in early October. Tommy's first competitive goal for the club had come in the second leg of the first round in the League Cup against Swindon Town in early September and the Greens booked themselves a date with the mighty Arsenal in the next round. After drawing 1–1 in an excellent match at Highbury on 4 October, they were narrowly beaten 1–0 at Home Park in front of 22,640 fans. For Tommy, it was the start of a run of seven games without a goal as the Greens picked up just 10 points. This poor run of results ended up with the dismissal of Bobby Moncur, who was replaced by former player John Hore on 1 October 1983.

It was Hore's first managerial job in professional football and Tommy remembers how he seemed to be in awe of the place. As a player he had become a legend at Home Park, playing 233 games and scoring 37 goals between 1965 and 1975. Born in Foxhole near St Austell in 1947, he made Argyle history on 31 August 1965. A new rule was passed to allow sides to bring on a substitute during a match and Hore became Argyle's first when he replaced the injured Frank Lord. On Boxing Day 1967 he played against QPR and all hell broke loose when Rodney Marsh was awarded a penalty after Hore had 'tackled' him. The penalty resulted in a goal and a full-scale pitch invasion at Home Park. Hore was also involved in the friendly against Pelé's Santos in front of a packed Home Park on 14 March 1973. The Greens won by three goals to two, with Pelé scoring a penalty, but the match had very nearly been cancelled just before kick-off. Seeing a large crowd of just short of 38,000, Santos demanded another £2,500 and chairman Robert Daniel was blackmailed into paying as they would refuse to play otherwise. At half-time the Brazilians were 3–0 down and demanded that the referee be changed or there would be no second half. It was Pelé who went into the dressing room and managed to talk the players into coming back out. Hore and the boys managed to hold on in the second half, with Dowling, Rickard and Hitch scoring all of Argyle's goals in the first 45 minutes. Edu scored for Santos in the second half and Pelé got a penalty, but it was not enough and Argyle won in one of the biggest, and probably strangest, fixtures ever to be played at Home Park.

We have already mentioned that goals were not forthcoming for Tommy during the early part of his Plymouth career, and the one he scored against Brentford at Griffin Park on 15 November was only his fourth from 17 matches. All strikers go through barren periods in their careers, and it is something they just have to deal with. The team as a whole were not firing on all cylinders or functioning as a closed unit. They had only managed 15 goals in the League up to that point. The service Tommy was getting from midfield was not the best, and the crowd were on his back. When he joined Plymouth his career goals-to-games ratio was good, but soon there was trouble and it all came to a head when John Hore told him how he thought Tommy was a lucky player. He summoned all the players for a crisis meeting and Tommy remembers the whole squad squashing into his office like sardines for a dressing down from the manager. He asked every single player if they wanted to play for Plymouth Argyle and not one of them said no.

Tommy remembers:

> 'When he asked me if I wanted to play for the club I said to him, "Of course I want to play, but my family comes first." I explained to him that my family were my priority and if they were happy and I was making enough money for them to be comfortable, I would be happy. John turned around to me and literally said to me, "I don't give a shit about your family, Tommy" and we left it at that.'

Many footballers fail to settle in at a club as the sudden upheaval is never easy. If a player does manage to settle it is easier for them to concentrate on the football. Despite the problems they were having settling in the south-west, Tommy signed for Argyle because he wanted to play for the club and he wanted to make a name for himself. Fortunately, this was just the beginning of Tommy's amazing journey with the Greens as he then set off to prove the manager wrong.

Argyle limped on under Hore and recorded a decent 4–0 win on New Year's Eve when they trounced Southend United at Home Park. Tommy was among the goals once again, with the others coming from Kevin Hodges and Andy Rogers, as well as an own-goal from Southend. He followed this with another goal two days later against Walsall, but it was clear to see that things had not really changed for the better under the new manager. There had been no improvement in terms of quality of play and the gates were still down. With all the hardship Tommy had faced, plus the fact that his wife felt unsettled in the area, he would not have been judged if he had slapped in a transfer request. Newport County were having a half-decent season and John Aldridge was still grabbing the headlines for the Welshmen.

Things did begin to change, however, and Tommy celebrated his 12th goal, a penalty, in a match at Hull City on 25 February. They ended up winning 2–1, with Lindsey Smith scoring the other. By now the Argyle crowd had started to warm to him thanks to a vital penalty he scored in the FA Cup against his old club Newport County. Argyle needed a replay to get past Southend United in the first round after a 0–0 draw and Tommy popped up with a goal in a 2–0 win. Tommy definitely sees the Newport game as a turning point:

> *'Scoring the penalty against Newport just gave me a lift really. The Argyle crowd had been on my back for not getting goals and I think their attitude towards me changed after that game, and it definitely helped my confidence.'*

In the second round they were paired with non-League Barking, who put up a good fight. The Greens finally won the match 2–1 and they suddenly found themselves in the hat with the big boys for the third-round draw. As luck would have it, they were drawn against Newport at home in what was to be a real blood and thunder Cup tie.

John Aldridge opened the scoring for County in the 11th minute when Andy Rodgers played a ball that was far too long. It was intercepted by Neville Chamberlain, who lifted it down the centre and over Geoff Crudgington in the Plymouth goal for Aldridge to tap in. It was left to Kevin Hodges to provide the equaliser, although a blunder from John Uzzell in the 83rd minute made Newport's second and it looked like Plymouth were going out. But then, in the third minute of injury time, Argyle were awarded a penalty and the chance of a replay was suddenly very real. Tommy snatched up the ball and placed it on the penalty spot as the Argyle fans jeered at him. There was no way anyone else was taking this spot-kick. His heart was pounding as he stepped up and realised just how important this spot-kick was. It was not just a kick to keep the Greens in the Cup, it was a chance for him to win over the fans, and he could not afford to miss. Newport's goalkeeper, Mark Kendall, knew Tommy well and he guessed that his former teammate would drive the ball to the left. Fortunately, Tommy outwitted Kendall that day by putting it into the right-hand corner of the net for the equaliser. He guessed Kendall would expect him to go left so he changed his strategy and earned the club a replay. On 10 January he returned to Somerton Park and Andy Rogers scored the only goal of the match to put Argyle into the fourth round.

There was to be no big team in the next round either, as instead they were drawn against Fourth Division Darlington in a home match, which was witnessed by almost 9,000 fans. The Greens were expected to win and they did not disappoint, beating them 2–1 and setting up a glamour tie with five-time Cup winners West Bromwich Albion of the First Division. Promoted in 1976, West Brom had had some decent finishes in the top flight and they were expected to win comfortably at the Hawthorns. The match took place on Saturday 18 February and West Brom were welcoming back former Manchester United, Leeds and Eire international player Johnny Giles as their manager. Although Giles did not contribute to the match programme, Albion were clearly happy that he was returning and were predicting the beginning of a new era – which saw them relegated two seasons later. The beginning of 1984 had seen the Baggies win two, draw one and lose three before the return of Giles, and they had been beaten 5–0 by Nottingham Forest at home 10 days earlier. Former Tottenham manager Martin Jol was playing for them that day, alongside the likes of Derek Statham and Tony Morley, but it was not to be Johnny Giles's day. It took less than 10 minutes for Argyle to break down the class barrier and it was difficult to see them as the underdogs.

By half-time the home team were beginning to fade, but it was not until the 58th minute that former Argyle 'keeper Paul Barron made a crucial mistake when he left his line to intercept a forward pass from Leigh Cooper just outside the goal area. With a burst of speed Gordon Staniforth beat Barron to the ball and slanted it back across the box. Tommy came steaming in from outside the penalty area and collected the pass on his chest. The two Albion defenders could not get anywhere near him and he propelled a first-time drive into the back of the net. Plymouth Argyle were through to the quarter-finals of the FA Cup and Tommy made the national newspapers once again with headlines like 'Terror Tom ruins the party' and 'Tynan's special agent'. Argyle may have been the underdogs, but Tommy believes they deserved the win:

> *'We knew we had a job on our hands against Albion, because they were a couple of Leagues higher than us and teams are unpredictable when a new manager comes in. I just think we were up for it from the off. There was no pressure on us and we were the better team on the day.'*

Soon it was back to reality for Plymouth and the serious business of picking up points in the League. By now the tide had turned and the fans were singing Tommy's name on the terraces. After a win against Hull City in the League they were beaten by Sheffield United and Bristol Rovers, and then only managed a point at home to Brentford, so a relegation dogfight was very much on the cards.

Just short of 35,000 flocked into Home Park on 10 March for the quarter-final against Second Division Derby County, whose miserable season would end in relegation. Derby 'keeper Steve Cherry kept the Rams in the game as he pulled off some outstanding saves in a match that ended goalless. Argyle's Gordon Staniforth came close to scoring when he hit a shot so hard that it bounced off the left-hand post and travelled right along the line before bouncing off the other post. For the replay, Derby manager Peter Taylor stated in his programme notes that the Rams had been lucky to survive but that the replay at the Baseball Ground would be thrills all the way as the magic of the FA Cup spread its wings over the game. Argyle took a decent amount of supporters with them, but the total attendance was around 8,000 short of the crowd at Home Park. Derby were third from bottom at the time and although Taylor was trembling with excitement at the chance of reaching the last four, it took just 17 minutes for Argyle to score the only goal of the match, and what a goal it was; a complete fluke, the scorer said after the game. Andy Rogers took Argyle's first corner and it went straight into the back of the net. The players were elated, and quietly spoken Chris Harrison was singing and leaping around in front of the Argyle fans like he was demented. When the final whistle was blown there were some pretty emotional scenes on the pitch and some of the Argyle players were so choked with tears that they could not speak to the media. Lindsey Smith stood with his fist clenched in a salute as John Hore ran over to congratulate his players. Derby's Scottish international Archie Gemmill trudged off the pitch with his head down, too dejected to talk to anybody. For the first time in their history, Third Division Plymouth Argyle were in the last four of the FA Cup, and the beers soon started to flow.

Argyle got back to the business of picking up League points with a 1–1 draw against Wigan on 3 April, which was the second of five successive League matches in which Tommy scored. His first goal came against Rotherham on 30 March, then came goals against Wigan, Scunthorpe and Wimbledon. On 16 April he scored in their final match of the season as the Greens lost 2–1 to Bolton Wanderers, but by then they were safe, finishing sixth from bottom with 51 points and 56 goals. They were five points clear of Scunthorpe United, who occupied the final relegation place. Exeter City finished bottom and Port Vale, Southend and Scunthorpe were all relegated alongside them. Argyle had survived by five points, but they recorded their lowest finish since 1978.

Elsewhere in football, Liverpool won the First Division for the third time in a row, finishing with three more points than Southampton. It was to be the best finish for the Saints since 1921 and they did well to beat Nottingham Forest to second place. Wolves, Notts County and Birmingham were all relegated from the top flight in 1984, to be replaced by Chelsea, Sheffield Wednesday and Newcastle United. Swansea City were relegated from Division Two, Lincoln City finished five places higher than Argyle and Rotherham finished one place and three points above the Greens. Doncaster Rovers were promoted from Division Four, Torquay finished ninth and Chester City finished bottom with just 34 points, which just about rounds up all of the professional clubs that Tommy was involved with. Liverpool recorded a League and League Cup double that year when Graeme Souness scored the only goal against Everton in a replay of the Final at Maine Road.

On Saturday 14 April 1984 Plymouth Argyle took part in the biggest game they have ever been involved in. There were just short of 44,000 people packed into Villa Park and the stadium was lit with brilliant sunshine. Inside there was a kaleidoscope of colour, the green and white of Plymouth against the yellow and red of Watford. Watford were backed by Elton John, and their manager Graham Taylor told the pop icon to keep 19 May free in his diary, he was that sure of a victory against the Greens. Despite Taylor's words, there was no way Tommy and the boys were going to lie down. They arrived at the ground to be greeted by hoards of reporters pointing cameras and microphones at them, all wanting exclusives and predictions for the forthcoming match. It was one of the best semi-finals for many years, with both teams having their fair share of chances. Argyle came close to scoring early on when a cruel dip and a curved shot just missed the Watford goal, and Nisbet and Staniforth began to terrorise the defence. Staniforth wriggled out of a corner on the right-hand side of the box and planted the ball in to Kevin Hodges, leaving Watford 'keeper Steve Sherwood totally confused. Hodges was convinced that his shot was going in, but the swerving ball bounced outside the woodwork. In the 13th minute England winger John Barnes picked up a stray pass from Leigh Cooper. Nisbet was caught out of position and Barnes sped off down the left flank. Six-foot-four George Reilly towered above the Argyle defence, and he was just far enough ahead of Lindsey Smith to connect with Barnes's inch-perfect cross and it ended up in the net. With their fingers burned and 1–0 down, Argyle became pretty effective at closing Barnes and Reilly down, but not before Crudgington was forced to make a vital save from Reilly in the 18th minute. Argyle continued to raise their game and Tommy kept drilling the ball through the middle, while Andy Rogers's ball skills and constant running threatened to overshadow Barnes and Callaghan out on the flanks. Argyle had a whole host of chances, including a shot from Tommy going over and a charging attempt from Cooper being diverted for a corner. Hodges connected with his head but the shot flashed inches over. It could easily have been 2–0 to the Hornets in the closing stages of the first half when John Uzzell's glancing header across the Argyle goalmouth caused panic. Not beaten yet, Argyle maintained the pressure into the second half while Tommy dummied an Andy Rogers cross early on. Staniforth received the ball but only managed to drive it into the arms of the 'keeper. After a while the Third Division team began to tire and their passing deteriorated. When the final whistle came, they had given their all but they had not pulled it off. Looking back on the match, Tommy says:

'It was a massive day for us and it was worth a few quid. Villa Park was full with fans dressed in green and white, and Elton John had turned up as well. It was a good game and we had more than our share of chances, but at the end of the day it just wasn't meant to be.'

In the end Everton lifted the trophy that year, beating the Hornets 2–0 at Wembley, with the goals coming from Graeme Sharp and Andy Gray. Argyle did not disgrace themselves at all that day and also managed to swell the coffers by an estimated £80,000.

The 1983–84 campaign turned out to be a pretty bizarre season for the Plymouth team. How could they have enough quality to do so much giant-killing and come within 90 minutes of the FA Cup Final, yet only narrowly avoid relegation into the Fourth Division for the first time in their history? Nobody could have questioned Hore's commitment to the club. He loved the place but it is fair to say that he did not do a great job as manager.

Chapter 15
A Young Boy Watching a Legend

After narrowly missing out on relegation the previous season, John Hore and his men were hoping for a drastic improvement and to mount a serious promotion challenge. With his goals and performances, Tommy was the jewel in Argyle's crown.

Things seemed much simpler back in the mid-1980s than at football matches today. At half-time the windows in the snack bars at the back of the stands would be steamed up by ever-brewing tea and all that could be seen inside were hunched silhouettes waving spoons or bagging up pasties for half-time consumption. The smell of Bovril was sometimes overpowering and fans had to mind they were not stood where a drunken docker had relieved himself. There was no under-soil heating or the sheltered corner of the stands of today either. If it was raining the faithful under the Lyndhurst terracing stayed dry, but those down the front, in the away end or in parts of the Devonport or Mayflower, got soaked right through. Being down the front of the Mayflower Terrace used to be the worst place to be, as the rain came right in. Fans could always go up into the Lyndhurst, but this meant standing on tiptoes in front of chain-smoking blokes in their knitted green jumpers. In the bad old days, when the football was particularly shocking, people threatened not to come back, but they always returned, no matter how much they cursed about the ball being launched when it should be played on the ground. It was unreal how, season after season, there were the same old faces.

Sometimes fans must have asked themselves why they were there, when they could have been at home in the warm. It took a while to understand the game and get over the disappointment of conceding vital goals in the very last minute, which Argyle seemed to do a fair bit of. After a while, each fan began to understand the mentality of the crowd. There was shared grief, like after the last-minute equaliser for Everton in the Cup, the collectiveness of the crowd sharing the pain and disappointment. That was what it was all about: waiting for that special moment, that flash of inspiration and the odd attempt at a bicycle-kick goal. At any moment events could turn around and that man Tynan would do something extraordinary with the ball, and disappointment turned to elation.

Special players like Tommy did emerge, but they were few and far between at Home Park and so all eyes would be on those elite few to provide the spark and ignite the team. Argyle were lacking this spark before his arrival; they needed a Wilf Carter or a Paul Mariner and for a good number of seasons the catalyst was not there. When Tommy started scoring for fun, the pressure he must have been under as he carried everybody's hopes and dreams must have been immense.

The goals he went on to score during the 1984–85 season would earn him the Divisional Golden Boot that year and he created more than his fair share of headlines. There were a number of top-flight clubs who were interested in securing his services over the next couple of seasons, including Chelsea, who were managed by Ian Porterfield at the time, but for one reason or another the big transfer never happened, so he just kept on doing what he did best, which was scoring goals.

The 1984–85 season started away to Burnley and, thanks to a Kevin Hodges goal, the Pilgrims picked up their first point of the season in front of a crowd of 6,613. They followed this with a win against local rivals Torquay in the first round of what was then the Milk Cup. After a home defeat to Reading, they went to Torquay for the second leg and came away with the same result. Tommy scored his first goal of the season up at Lincoln in a match that ended 2–2 on 8 September. They then earned just two points from the next three matches and were thumped 7–2 by Bolton on the 22nd, with Tommy scoring one of the consolation goals. He hit another in Argyle's first League win on the 29th as they battered Preston 6–4, with the Argyle fans jumping the barrier at the end. Apart from the goal, his best contribution came when he played a fantastic cross to Kevin Hodges after intercepting from Andy Roger, with Hodges smacking the ball into the back of the net for Argyle's third. Tommy managed another in the next match against Gillingham and then they were knocked out of the Cup by Birmingham City on 9 October, losing 1–0 on the night and 5–1 on aggregate. By the time Tommy scored two in a 4–3 defeat up at Doncaster, Argyle had managed just two League wins from their first 13 matches, and this signalled the end of John Hore's time in charge. Tommy had managed seven goals from those games but the best was yet to come. Hore was finally sacked in late November and replaced by Scotsman Dave Smith.

Hore was a different beast to the gentlemanly Bobby Moncur, and despite what Hore had to say to him Tommy believes that after the Cup run he should have been given more time to sort out the team.

Smith was like a breath of fresh air for Argyle, and he had an almost immediate effect on the team. He took charge for the first time on 24 November 1984, and in his first match against Walsall at Home Park, despite another goal from Tommy they were beaten 3–1 in front of a crowd just short of 5,000. The next game saw Tommy returning to the Vetch Field in a match described by Smith as one of the 10 best games he had been involved in. Argyle were absolutely outstanding that day, and they ended up beating Swansea City 2–0 with goals coming from Tommy and Clive Goodyear. After drawing 0–0 with Hereford in the second round of the FA Cup, Cambridge United came to Home Park and the Pilgrims did it again. A flash of brilliance from Kevin Hodges set up the first goal early on and then at the end of the match, after a long wait and some missed opportunities, Tommy pounced once again and scored goal number 12 for the season. He followed this with a hat-trick against Bristol City on Boxing Day, but it was not quite enough as City won the match 4–3 up at Ashton Gate. Argyle ended the year with a defeat at Newport, but Smith had earned nine points and won three of his first five League matches, taking Argyle's total number of wins for the season so far to six from 22 League matches.

Tommy started 1985 with a vital goal in a 1–1 draw against Brentford on New Year's Day. By 2 February Argyle had picked up another four points from two games. On 9 February Bolton Wanderers were beaten 2–0 by Argyle who, early on in the game, showed they were well disciplined in an otherwise drab encounter. Tommy pounced early on, scoring a cracking goal in the 16th minute, with Clive Goodyear getting the second.

By the time Mikhail Gorbachev became the new leader of the USSR on 11 March, Argyle had picked up another eight points from five games. Tommy put in another outstanding performance against his future team Rotherham United when they beat them away on the ninth in front of just over 4,000 fans. At the time Rotherham were still in with a chance of promotion and Tommy's performance that day certainly turned a few heads. Dave Smith decided to change things around: Argyle started the match with two wingers and the team were given the instruction to attack. As the match wore on, the travelling Argyle fans could see what their team were trying to do and they urged them on by singing 'attack-attack-attack-attack-attack'. They were rewarded with two goals, both from the wing.

Andy Rogers had a hand in the first as he sped up the flank early on, his pass found Kevin Summerfield and they were 1–0 up after just nine minutes. Argyle continued to batter Rotherham, who could not cope with the Pilgrims' pace. Their defence was finally reduced to rubble when a six-man move ended up at the feet of Tommy, who whacked the ball into the net for his 20th of the season, and he felt on top of the world. Scoring a goal in a professional football match is one thing, but after hitting the landmark 20th goal he was absolutely thrilled.

Before any inkling of a transfer became apparent, there were still another 15 games for Tommy to play for Argyle after the match against Rotherham and another 12 goals for him to score. His next came against promotion-chasing Gillingham on 19 March at Home Park and they drew 2–2. In the next match, an away draw with Hull City (who would be promoted that season), he got both. One of them came early and it was a shock to Hull, who came back strongly. Chance after chance came for the Tigers, and by half-time they were 2–1 up. Instead of having their confidence knocked, whatever Dave Smith said to his team in the dressing room at half-time did the trick. Much better at man-management than his predecessor, the self-styled 'Cyderman' was a fantastic bloke with great people skills and he liked to spout the odd line of poetry too. In the second minute of the second half Tommy collected a pass from Andy Rogers and beat Hull 'keeper Tony Norman with a fantastic shot to level the score. Argyle managed to hold out and returned home with a well-earned point. In the very next game at Home Park Tommy hit two more against Burnley in another 2–2 draw, and the next two games saw Argyle pick up three more points so they were looking good for a mid-table finish. Tommy scored five from the next four matches and he was truly having the time of his life on the pitch as the goals came thick and fast. After getting another against Swansea City, he scored his last for Argyle from the penalty spot against

Cambridge United on 4 May 1985. There were two League matches remaining and Argyle picked up another three points to finish in 15th position in Division Three, and Tommy's 32 goals from 52 games in all competitions (45 appearances and 31 goals in the League) has not been bettered since. In total, Argyle scored 62 goals in the League, with Tommy scoring 50 per cent of that final total. It is interesting to note that without him that season Argyle would have finished with just 42 points and been placed second from bottom, rather than with their end total of 59. That was how vital Tommy was to the club. That season he won the Golden Boot and was named club Player of the Year.

Despite the problems the Tynans were experiencing settling in Plymouth, Tommy was still prepared to enter negotiations with Argyle over a new contract for the next season. When the club refused to give him any more money he made up his mind to move on. He had not had a pay rise during his time at Argyle. The Argyle supporters were devastated when the news broke. It had taken Tommy a while to settle in at Home Park but by the time he left the crowd loved him and saw him as their own.

When contract talks between Argyle and Tommy broke down at the end of the 1984–85 season, Tommy talked to a couple of teams about a move. Second Division Middlesbrough were interested but nothing came of it, and they were relegated at the end of the next season so it was probably a good thing that the move did not happen. The next offer came from a man mentioned previously, and Tommy travelled to London, expenses paid, to meet him. Scotsman George Graham was to go on and do great things with Arsenal, but in 1986 he was in charge of Millwall, who would be in the top flight two years later. Tommy was very impressed with what he saw and Graham pulled out all the stops. Millwall had just won promotion from the Third Division and were keen to sign a proven goalscorer, and Tommy would have been the right kind of player for Graham.

However, they were unable to offer him any more money than he was on at Argyle and told him to go away and have a think about it, but his mind was already made up. It was quite obvious that he and his family's standard of living would worsen in the capital city so the move never happened. When Rotherham manager Norman Hunter offered him what he wanted, Tommy signed up. After relegation from the Second Division in 1983 Rotherham United had struggled during their first season back in the Third Division and they finished seventh from bottom (one place higher than Argyle). They eventually finished the 1984–85 campaign in 12th place, but they were one of the lowest scoring sides that year. However, Tommy felt a move back up north was good for his family so the Tynans moved back to Sheffield to be closer to their family and friends. Millmoor was not the footballing capital of the world, but neither was it as dilapidated as some of the grounds Tommy had played at during the last 15 years.

The Dallas Tornadoes team of 1976.

Elaine and Tommy.

Argyle 6 Huddersfield Town 1, August 1987.

Tommy Tynan: The Original 'Football Idol'.

A hat-trick for the captain against Stoke City in September 1988.

Playing against Hull City in the same season.

Up against a young Dean Holdsworth.

Doing the business against top-flight QPR in a pre-season friendly in 1989.

Tommy in 1989, approaching the end of his time at Argyle. In his last season at the club he scored 18 goals, and Argyle have never had such a consistent goalscorer since he left.

Tommy's Testimonial in 1991 with Thomas Jnr (centre), Jordanna (front right) and Paul Staplehous's children, Ollie (far left) and Amy (second right).

Tommy and Elaine on their wedding day, 17 July 1982.

A boat trip in Plymouth in 1984.

Lockington Avenue in 1988. Left to right: Jordanna, Tommy, Thomas Jnr, Elaine, Keeley.

Holidaying in Tenerife in 1988.

From left to right: Grandson Mason, son Thomas and Tommy on holiday in Turkey.

Dinner and entertainment for Plymouth Argyle at the Continental Hotel.

Jordanna, Tommy and Keeley at Elaine's 50th held at Stoke Social Club on 7 July 2001.

The family on holiday in Majorca in 1982. Left to right: Tammy, Jordanna, Elaine, Tommy and Keeley.

The family on holiday in Corfu in 1990.

Left: Tommy, Keeley and Elaine. Right: Thomas, Tammy and Jordanna.

Tommy in Corfu.

Tommy in front of the great 'Jumbo' Chisholm.

Chapter 16
To Rotherham and Back

It was a transfer that should never have happened. Tommy had completed two extremely successful seasons at Argyle and his contract had come to an end. When other clubs got wind that a deal could not be struck at Plymouth, the feelers were out. Tommy did not think he was being unreasonable when he asked Argyle for an improved contract and he was not asking for massive amounts of cash. When you consider how short a player's career can be, without even considering the possibility of an injury, his request does not seem to have been out of order. It must be remembered that when Tommy was playing the club held the players' registrations, so even at the end of a contract they were still the property of the club. The Bosman ruling was still many years away, so the club was very much in on the deal when an out-of-contract player moved to another club. Today, a player is entitled to a 'free transfer' and they can discuss their own terms. The power base has moved and some may argue that the balance has now swung too far in favour of the player. It is not uncommon to see a player who does not care about the club they join as his agent strikes a deal with whoever is offering the most money. This, as they say, is progress, and loyalty to a club is a rarity, but thankfully there are still characters around like Steve Bull, Matthew Le Tissier and Ryan Giggs who all stayed loyal to their clubs.

In 1893 Rotherham Town finished second from bottom in the Second Division. It was their first season in the professional Leagues and only Northwich Victoria finished below them. From 28 matches Rotherham managed just 15 points, scored 44 and conceded a massive

91 goals against the likes of Liverpool, Newcastle United and Woolwich Arsenal, who were all playing in the same League. Northwich Victoria's only League season ended in disaster as the Londoners finished bottom with just nine points and conceded 98 goals as they vanished into the lower Leagues. Rotherham faired no better in their second season but this time it was Crewe Alexandra who kept them off the bottom of the table. Dropping out of the League at the end of the season, Rotherham failed to regain their League status until well into the new century. As Rotherham County, they finished 17th in Division Two in 1920 and they were relegated to Division Three North in 1923. Two years later they finished bottom of Division Three North and changed their name to 'United' the following season. They were finally promoted as champions in 1951 and spent a couple of seasons challenging for the top flight during the early 1950s before being relegated alongside Argyle in 1968. They experienced their first season of Division Four football in 1974, but they were back in the Third Division for a couple of seasons in 1975. Six years later they were promoted as champions, and when Tommy put pen to paper in the summer of 1985 they were preparing for their third season in the Third Division.

With legendary Leeds United player Norman Hunter in charge, Rotherham were looking for a quick return to the Second Division and bought Tommy in July 1985 to help with the low scoring record of the previous season. Hunter knew he was getting the 29-year-old for a very decent price, Tommy's fitness levels were good and he played the type of game Rotherham wanted to play. Hunter had played with some of the greats during his time at Leeds United and he knew Tommy was the type of player who, given a good supply, was capable of blowing defences apart. He was more than capable of scoring his quota of goals for the team and if he got the chance to play his own game (and not be forced into a roll he was uncomfortable with) he possessed extraordinary ability. There is not a manager in the game who would not have wished they possessed a player of such skill, and it is in the hope of finding such a player that a manager will shell out a lot of money. In Tynan, Hunter had a proven goalscorer and he had not cost Rotherham United the earth.

Hunter knew Tommy still had a good few years of goalscoring in front of him if he could do all of the above and keep him fit. He had seen him pick his team apart the previous season with a well-taken goal, but he was also impressed with the way Tommy led the line and received vital passes. He could often fool the opposition, making it seem as if he was just a couple of steps ahead of everybody else on the pitch. He could lay the ball off or play a tight angled pass through a melee of limbs, as well as being deadly in the box. His pure muscle and pinpoint accuracy often saw him coming from nowhere and, like the knockout punch the boxer fails to see, his close control and quick turns usually ended in a goal. In the beginning it all went swimmingly; Tommy was exactly what was promised. For the best part of the season everything was working and he notched up 17 goals from 39 matches for Rotherham, but, despite the hopes of the fans, there would not be a quick return to the Second Division.

Tommy was fortunate to settle in at Rotherham pretty quickly. His family were happy to be back home in Sheffield and soon a baby brother came along for the three sisters, Tammy, Keeley and Jordanna. Thomas Jnr came into the world on 18 September, a month after Tommy's first match for Rotherham United. On 17 August they drew 1–1 with Bolton Wanderers. A week later they recorded their first home win when they beat Lincoln City, before they were thrashed by Second Division Sheffield United over two legs in the League Cup. Tommy's first goal came from the penalty spot at home to Bristol City on the 31st. During his next six matches Rotherham managed just seven points, but he did get the consolation goal on 5 October when they were beaten 2–1 by Wolverhampton Wanderers (who were on their way to relegation) at home.

Despite Rotherham's indifferent form, Tommy was still doing the business and the Argyle fans were gutted to see him score against them at Home Park on 2 November in a match that ended in a 1–1 draw. His next goal came against Bury on 23 November and he scored his last of 1985 against Bournemouth in mid-December, with Rotherham managing a win this time. He scored one against Bristol City, two against Bolton Wanderers and a hat-trick against his old club Swansea City on 1 February. However, just as he was hitting a particularly rich vein of form that saw him score 17 goals from 16 League matches (seven of those were for Rotherham), things went horribly wrong and his last game for Rotherham came on 1 March when they were beaten 2–1 by Brentford.

During one of Rotherham's training sessions Hunter decided to have a five-a-side match, which was a little bit too physical for Tommy's liking as tackles were flying in like it was a real match. The final straw came when fellow player Phil Crosby went in for a particularly nasty challenge on Tommy and then turned and shouldered him out of the way:

> 'I have to admit that I was absolutely seething and, in a rush of blood, I headbutted the lad, but it wasn't like I planned to do it or anything, we were supposed to be teammates and he was having a go at me out there. Unfortunately, I just caught him in the wrong place and blood poured out of his head and they had to take him to hospital to have some stitches. It was just one of those spur of the moment incidents, the red mist descended and I just reacted. I had always got on with Phil and this was only a training match. Why he decided to shoulder me out of the way is anybody's guess. Norman Hunter saw things differently and the next day he took me into the office and said he'd had a sleepless night and that he was placing me on the transfer list. I told him if that was what he wanted to do then it was fine by me, but he

should remember that two players had been involved in the incident. Hunter didn't want to know and he stuck me in the reserves, telling me his decision was final. The thing that annoyed me was that he [Hunter] told me that we would keep the incident to ourselves and that he wasn't going to go to the papers, which is exactly what he did do.'

The next thing Tommy knew the Press were on his case and *The Sun* and *The Express* were running stories about a 'fight' between the manager and player. Phil Crosby was not even mentioned. Reporters were hassling Tommy to tell them what had happened between him and Hunter, and he said he would give them a story if they spoke to Hunter first. When the Press found out what had really happened they had a field day, but to be fair to Crosby he did tell them what had really happened on the training ground. Whether Hunter had gone to the Press first is unknown. What did happen is that the story Crosby gave to *The Sun* reporter was twisted around and people believed that there had been a physical fight. The truth finally came out when Tommy made a statement. Norman Hunter now wanted him out and told him he would never play for Rotherham United again. Dave Smith, on the other hand, was more than happy to have Tommy back for the rest of the season and, of the nine clubs who were trying to get him on loan, Smith was the man Tommy wanted to play for so he was soon welcomed back to Home Park with open arms. Smith met Tommy at a service station on the M5 and a deal was done. Shortly after he rejoined, Argyle defender Gordon Nisbet had a premonition about the future and went on record welcoming Tommy back, telling the Press that no one would be more pleased than him if he could score 10 goals and the team win promotion.

Chapter 17

The Boy is Back in Town: Bristol City and all that

With nine games to go in the 1985–86 season, Argyle hovered around the top of the League, but promotion was by no means a certainty. The fans were pleased to have Tommy back and for his first game he travelled with the team to mid-table Bournemouth for what could have been a tricky encounter. Tommy was equally pleased to be back with Argyle, and wanted the game against Bournemouth to herald a new successful chapter to his career.

> 'It had turned out to be a bloody nightmare at Rotherham, and although we had to uproot once again and leave Sheffield we knew we had to give it our all. I was in my 30s by now and was determined to finish on a high.'

Before the match the mood in the changing room was buoyant and Smith's team were full of confidence. In front of 5,351 at Dean Court, Tommy wore the green shirt once again and Argyle took command of the game from the very first minute, putting on an excellent attacking display. Steve Cooper opened the scoring in the 12th minute and Russell Coughlin made it two with a clinically executed penalty just before the half-time whistle. Argyle had struggled to find the rhythm of the first half for a while and Steve Cooper and Darren Rowbotham both missed golden opportunities. The team were a little unsettled in the early part of the second half, and Bournemouth threatened to get one back as they stepped up the pace and played a more aggressive game. Bournemouth's newly invigorated play looked good, but it never really came to anything and the only real threat came from Colin Clarke, but John Uzzell did a decent job of dominating him most of the time. It got a little scary for the Greens when Beck pulled one back in the 72nd minute, but they kept their nerve and Kevin Hodges sealed the win six minutes before the end. Argyle were comfortable in fourth position, despite the fact that Derby County were just behind them in the League and they still had a couple of games in hand.

The crowd gave Tommy a rapturous welcome on his home debut as the team ran out to the familiar sound of *Tempris Fidelis*. Tommy was lining up against the club who held his registration, and Argyle hammered Hunter's men 4–0. Despite the fact he was still a Rotherham player, Tommy never believed he would play for them again and from the start of the match he set out to prove a point. The Pilgrims' fiery determination left the Millers reeling, and Pickering conceded a goal in the 17th minute to give Argyle the lead. Rotherham did not really pose too much of a threat, but Argyle were a little too frantic, with nine of their 22 shots missing the target and numerous key passes going wayward. Tommy hit his first in the 33rd minute and he got another in the 59th, which left Norman Hunter reeling. In the dying minutes Smith replaced Garry Nelson (who was suffering with a viral infection) with Kevin Summerfield and he made it 4–0 almost instantly. Just over 13,000 fans turned up that Tuesday night to witness the mauling, but Smithy was not happy with Hodges, who had played the match with his socks rolled down and had shown a real lack of discipline. Norman Hunter was so angry about Tommy being involved in the match that the Press got yet another story about a supposed 'gentlemen's agreement' which, Hunter claimed, existed between the two clubs. The truth is, when Dave Smith took Tommy on loan he phoned Hunter and asked him if he could play him against Rotherham, and Hunter had said he would get back to him about it. Hunter and his assistant, Bobby Claxon, just wanted rid of Tommy after the training ground incident and they were not really interested in what happened to him, until he helped demolish Rotherham and move the Greens into second in the League. Smith's call to Hunter was never returned and the rest, as they say, is history.

Next it was Bury's turn to pit their wits against Argyle at fortress Home Park. Under player-manager Martin Dobson, they were struggling and were sitting fourth from bottom, despite having 21-year-old Lee Dixon in defence that day. It was not Argyle's greatest performance, but their commitment was faultless and they showed good tactical awareness and dominated the game for long periods. They could easily have scored five or six goals, although Bury did cause them a few problems. Argyle looked dangerous but Bury hustled them and succeeded in making the Greens look ragged at times. John Matthews and Russell Coughlin ended up with a warning for being a little too over-aggressive, and Kevin Hodges opened the scoring in the 12th minute. In the 30th minute Tommy found a gap between the defender and goalkeeper Phil Hughes to score Argyle's second. In the 59th he was at it again and his powerful shot from just inside the area beat the 'keeper and Argyle won the game 3–0 and stayed in second place.

On Wednesday 16 April Tommy returned to Sincil Bank and Argyle started poorly against Lincoln City. From the off they were defending corners and free-kicks, and Lincoln were a goal up after just three minutes. Argyle started to find their shape after a while and came back strongly, attacking for long periods of time. For 15 minutes they put Lincoln under immense pressure and the ball was never out of their half of the pitch. However, once again they were too frantic and the finishing was not good. They had done everything they could in the first half but they could not score. At half-time Dave Smith gave the players a talking to about finishing, positioning and technique, urging them to keep up the momentum. After 10 minutes of the second half the story was just the same and it did not look like it was going to be Argyle's day. But then, in the 54th minute, Tommy came from nowhere and slammed the ball into the back of the net for the equaliser, and the Pilgrims went home with a point and remained in second spot. Tommy clearly remembers the pressure the squad was under to continue their good form:

> *'Nobody can deny that we had a decent side, but at times we were a bit rough around the edges as we had so much at stake. Nobody wanted to miss out, especially me. I was trying to turn the loan into a permanent transfer.'*

The wheels finally came off at Wigan on 19 April and Argyle were beaten 3–0 in a game that saw the Latics going for the player rather than the ball. Things did not settle until they scored their first, but Argyle did not have a chance and alarm bells started to ring as they slipped to fourth in the League. Three days later, they hoped to make up for dropping five points from their last two matches and they got back to their best against Bolton Wanderers in front of a home crowd of 15,000. A win was vitally important and Argyle dominated from start to finish in a match played at a 'fever pitch' tempo. Bolton took an undeserved lead in the 17th minute, but Argyle sustained the power, presence and sheer quality of their crosses. Despite all of their dominant play, with less than 20 minutes remaining Argyle were still one down. In a match many still remember, the Greens scored four goals in the last 18 minutes, with three of those goals coming in the last five minutes. Kevin Hodges hit the equaliser after 72 minutes, much to the relief of the crowd, who were just starting to contemplate another season of Third Division football. In the 85th minute Russell Coughlin converted a penalty, and a tremendous piece of finishing from Tommy a minute later made it 3–1. Bolton just wanted to get back on the coach and go home, but before they could do this Adrian Burrows made it four in the very last minute. The Lyndhurst End exploded and Argyle moved back up to third.

On 26 April it was the turn of Blackpool, and they dominated the match from the off. They won nearly every loose ball and got everything in the air front and back. At half-time Blackpool were 1–0 up and Smithy gave the boys a telling-off, which must have done the trick because the team seemed to grow in strength as the second half progressed. It was really windy and the pitch was like concrete, but things were starting to look up. Garry Nelson got the equaliser in the 50th minute, Russell Coughlin got another penalty 18 minutes later and Tommy got one right at the death to make it 3–1 to the Greens. They remained in third place and everyone knew that a win against Bristol City in the penultimate game of the season would mean promotion, but nobody dared utter the word. The Blackpool match had not been Argyle's best display but they had shown that they were able to stand up to the more physical teams. Smithy liked to mix the long ball in with the play, but Argyle's versatility showed and Tommy rates the side as the best he ever played for. They had pace and skill, as well as the strength of 'Rambo' McElhinney knitting the players together at the back and showing some of the younger lads the way forward.

Plymouth Argyle 4 Bristol City 0, 29 April 1986

The floodlights seemed that bit brighter and the crowd even more passionate that day, willing the ball into the back of the net. Umbrella Vi was on the edge of the crowd, whirling her 'Argyle' brolly for all she was worth. The old lady was Argyle's lucky mascot and she had become a local celebrity. Little children sitting at the front of the Lyndhurst and Devonport Ends would turn to watch as she waved her brolly like some football mad Mary Poppins whenever the players celebrated a goal.

There are many moments from the promotion season of 1985–86 which have become imprinted onto the minds of those who witnessed the games, but none so deeply as that night and those goals, when the Greens overturned the Reds and the chant of 'Argyle till I die' rang out through the ground. In the town centre people stopped and turned as they heard the crowd from miles away. Many of those who saw the match found themselves staring at the ceiling that night, full of adrenaline and unable to sleep, totally consumed with the knowledge that the Greens were going up!

> *'The City match stands out because of what it signified for the club and for myself. It was a terrific atmosphere and I managed to grab two goals myself. At the end, when we knew we were up, all I can remember is the crowd rushing at us from all sides. What a night!'*

From the off Bristol City were playing an attacking game and it was quite a tussle for the first 30 minutes, with nobody wanting to give anything away too early. The opposition were chasing the game for the first half an hour and that was exactly what Smith had anticipated. It was to be a massive Geoff Crudgington clearance that caught the City defenders off guard. Garry Nelson forced the bouncing ball into the penalty area and Tommy was waiting there to steer it past City 'keeper Waugh. The second came in the eighth minute of the second half and Tommy was in the middle of the pitch to receive the pass. In a second he flipped the ball up to Nelson who lobbed the 'keeper for the second. Argyle's third was a complete fluke. Waugh and Llewellen had managed to keep out a Kevin Summerfield shot for a corner. Russell Coughlin's long left swinger passed over a couple of City players and into the corner of the goal.

Nothing could be heard over the noise of the crowd. They could taste victory, but the best was yet to come. Garry Nelson lost the ball and Kevin Hodges managed to regain possession on the edge of the penalty area. He spun around and saw Tommy sprinting in. Tommy could see what he was trying to do. Hodges passed the ball and Tommy hurled himself forward for the fourth. Bristol City were unable to cope with the constant pressure and were soundly beaten. Argyle were finally on their way out of Division Three to take their place among the likes of Sunderland, Leeds United, Blackburn Rovers and Portsmouth. Tommy's return to Plymouth had been an inspired move, and he had more than lived up to the fans' expectations with his 10 goals (and there was still one to come against Darlington in the last game of the season which Argyle won 2–0).

It had not worked out at Rotherham, but the saga was not over yet. No one could have foreseen the rich vein of form Tommy had been in, and Norman Hunter must have been kicking himself. It helped Tommy to step into an Argyle team who were on fire, and he was delighted with his performance that night. After the game the city was alive, the pubs packed and the newspapers full of Dave Smith's team. Pictures flickered across millions of television sets showing the destruction of Bristol City and the full-time pitch invasion that followed. In an era when Chelsea chairman Ken Bates had erected barbed wire and electric fences to stop the crowd from getting on to the pitch, a victorious Argyle team were carried from the field of play by their fans.

Back in the days when a scout at a club with no money could spot a bit of talent and bring them in on the cheap, it was still possible to be successful without spending millions. Plymouth fans truly believed that their turn in the top flight was coming. They had seen teams like Oxford United, Luton Town and Watford mixing it with the big boys, and then Wimbledon, who were promoted to what is now the Premiership as Argyle took their place in the second tier. Both Oxford and Luton had some decent finishes in the League and both lifted the League Cup in the 1980s. With the first steps taken and promotion achieved, there was genuine belief in the south west that Dave Smith's Plymouth Argyle team could get promoted again and hold their own at the top. They had been close a couple of times in the past, but the diehard fans had been starved of success on the whole. Plymouth and Hull were at that time the only large cities in England whose teams had not represented them in the top flight.

Dave Smith's reorganisation stepped up a gear in the summer of 1986 as he plotted the campaign ahead with new coach Stewart Houston, who had come in to replace Martin Harvey. Since Smith had been at the club he had brought in players like John Matthews from Huddersfield; John Brimacombe from local team Saltash United; the late Steve Cooper from Newport County; John Clayton from Chesterfield and the influential Garry Nelson from Leyton Orient. Steve Cherry was on his way to compete for Crudgington's place and defender Nicky Law was signed before the transfer deadline. Stewart Evans was the other new face, but his performances were limited in the season ahead. Smith knew that Tommy's signature would be the final piece in the jigsaw, but his return to Home Park was not immediate. After being told there was no future for him at Rotherham United, he expected a move to happen over the summer. However, this did not happen and after the break he found himself reporting to Norman Hunter for pre-season training.

'Never in my wildest dreams could I have imagined I would be training with Rotherham again, let alone playing for the first team, but on my return Hunter did not say a word to me and he just got on with things. It was not until they held an open day and a question and answer session had been set up for the fans that I first spoke about the situation. I remember one fan decided to ask me why I was playing again after everything they had seen in the

papers. I told him that he should ask the manager and said nothing more. There is always one wise guy but I didn't want to stir it anymore. I don't want people to think I was trouble, I just wanted out. There was no going back and Hunter just blocked me out'

Rotherham started the new season at home to Fulham, drawing 0–0. Tommy played in the game and he also played in the League Cup matches against Doncaster Rovers, scoring two goals. He was involved in a 1–1 draw with Port Vale, but by then Dave Smith was busy brokering a deal behind the scenes. One afternoon Hunter called Tommy into the office and told him about the Argyle offer. It was so hush-hush that even the Argyle directors did not know about it, Smithy simply turned up in the middle of a board meeting with Tommy in tow and introduced them to their new signing before walking out. Fortunately they splashed the cash and Tommy rejoined Argyle for £25,000 in September 1986.

Chapter 18
Back to Stay

The Greens started the 1986–87 campaign well, with four points from their first two League games, but Cardiff City had battered them in the Cup and now, with Tommy returning, they faced Hull City. Kevin Summerfield had been given the number-nine shirt in his absence, and he had found the net twice but had been substituted against Cardiff in the first leg of the Cup game. Things had started pretty well in the League and they managed a point away to Bradford City in the first match, and a Kevin Hodges goal defeated Reading at home in front of 10,000 in the very next fixture. Apart from Tommy's absence, the team had changed little and the side seemed to be coping with the higher standard of football quite well. The win against Division Three Champions Reading on 30 August had given them a psychological boost, and the Royals finished below Argyle that year in 13th place. The new signings were settling in well and they were pulling out good enough results to keep them around the top of the table.

Tommy made his third debut for Argyle up at Boothferry Park on 6 September 1986. Both teams were desperate to defy the label they shared as underachievers, and, although Argyle had a good stab at promotion that year, Hull City were very nearly relegated. A crowd of 6,451 turned up to watch Argyle beat Hull 3–0. They had been promoted the season before Argyle but the match, like the season ahead, turned out to be a nightmare for the Tigers. Argyle looked confident, from the 'keeper right the way through the team to the centre-forwards, and the players seemed to be buzzing. Tommy lined up alongside Steve Cooper, whose style of play was sometimes a little rough around the edges but he loved nothing more than when the ball was in the air, and he was a commanding presence with a powerful header. Kevin Summerfield had been moved to midfield on Tommy's return, and what an impression he made. The opening goal came in the 13th minute and Summerfield was involved. His header went to Cooper and then to Leigh, who walloped it past 'keeper Tony Norman from 20 yards out. Russell Coughlin and John Matthews were threatening to run the show, with Coughlin playing a fantastic diagonal ball to Summerfield, much to the delight of the travelling Argyle fans. Leigh Cooper scored the second with an intricate string of passes, starting from the halfway line and catching Hull's defence square. Tommy ran wide before thumping the ball towards Cooper from the right wing, and he put it into the net with his head. Summerfield got the third with a controlled header that beat the 'keeper and Argyle were going home with the points.

They followed the win with a 2–2 draw at Home Park against Brighton & Hove Albion, who were to finish bottom that year, and almost 10,000 turned up to see Tommy's return. However, his first official goal came in a 3–2 defeat against Ipswich Town in the Full Members' Cup. Argyle managed a draw up at Barnsley, they then beat Blackburn Rovers at home and forged credible draws against Billy Bremner's Leeds United and then Grimsby Town, but Tommy still had not scored in his first six League games. Just like his first spell at Argyle, it took him a little bit of time to settle. He had been all over the place during the past year and this time, despite the distance from Sheffield, the Tynans were determined to make it work. Tommy scored his first League goal in a 1–0 win against Sheffield United at Home Park on 27 September in front of 11,000 people. He slid the ball past 'keeper John Burridge and Dave Smith was a happy man. In his programme notes Smith talked about raising their game to beat United and the win kept them in touch with the leaders. Tommy's next goal came in a 4–2 defeat against Sunderland at home as they recorded their biggest gate so far, with 13,482 attending on 21 October. They then beat Ipswich Town and lost at Millwall, before Tommy scored another brace in a 3–1 win against Crystal Palace.

West Bromwich Albion came to town on 15 November and they topped the attendance for the Sunderland game as 14,679 turned up to see Gordon Nisbet score the only goal of the game and keep the Pilgrims in touch with the top. Although they had squandered a few chances in front of goal, Argyle deserved the win and Nisbet's goal was a 25-yard thunderbolt that Tommy laid on from a Leigh Cooper free-kick. The shot left West Brom 'keeper Stuart Naylor helpless, and as the game wore on Argyle should have scored another two. John Clayton's shot was cleared off the line and Clive Goodyear's header went over the bar. They then beat Huddersfield away and Tommy got another, before they beat Oldham 3–2 at Home Park. Just over 17,000 turned up to see Argyle pit their wits against the League leaders and Joe Royle's team included youngsters Andy Goram, Dennis Irwin and Andy Linighan. It was a mistake by Linighan that led to Argyle's first goal after 10 minutes when he failed to cut out a pass down the centre from Tommy which was collected by John Clayton, who scored a cracker. Adrian Burrows got the second when Russell Coughlin's ball landed on his head, but Mike Milligan got one back for the Latics before Tommy headed home the third in the 61st minute. In the dying minutes Ron Futcher lobbed Crudgington for Oldham's second and his goal made the game look closer than it actually was.

December was a disappointing month for Argyle, who were in third spot on the 13th. They drew 1–1 with Derby County that day, with Tommy scoring the goal. However, out of the five League matches they had played that month they had taken just two points and Tommy had found the net only once. So far (with the exclusion of the Full Members' Cup) Tommy had played 20 matches and scored seven goals for Argyle, but 1987 would bring many more goals.

December had been bad but Argyle picked up nine points from 12 in January after starting the year with a 3–2 defeat up at St Andrews against Birmingham City. City had been relegated the previous season and narrowly avoided the drop once more as they finished 19th with two more points than Sunderland. Two down against the Blues, Argyle's first goal came from Clive Goodyear, who put the ball into the far corner of the net after John Matthews failed to put away a chance Tommy had set up for him. Towards the end Argyle nearly equalised when a Garry Nelson cross saw Tommy blast the ball across the face of the goal. Crudgington made a string of fine saves to keep them in the game, but Birmingham eventually got the third. Tommy popped up in the 86th minute to head home his first in four games, but it was still not quite enough, despite Nelson forcing the Birmingham 'keeper to make a vital save in the dying minutes to deny them a point.

On 3 January 1987 11,697 people flocked to Home Park and saw the Pilgrims beat Hull City 4–0. It was a match that showed off Tommy's heading ability and ended a run of six games without a win. Garry Nelson's right-wing corner found Adrian Burrows beyond the far post and he headed the ball towards the goal, where Tommy flicked a header over 'keeper Tony Norman in the 30th minute to make it 1–0. Five minutes later, he nodded the ball down for Kevin Hodges, who powered home a 25-yard shot to make it two. In the 60th minute he was in the thick of it once again when he knocked down Gordon Nisbet's right-winged cross and Nelson scored with a well-angled shot. Russell Coughlin created an opening 10 minutes later and Tommy wrapped it up with another header to make it four and end Plymouth's losing streak. He scored again in a 3–2 win against Bradford on 24 January before they went to Arsenal on the last day of the month for the fourth round of the FA Cup.

Despite all the hopes and dreams of the travelling fans, and the thousands listening to radios back home, the Gunners demolished

Argyle 6–1 in front of 39,000 people. A dream of Wembley and a win that seemed so definite was soon to be shattered as reality kicked in. The exclusion of goalkeeper Geoff Crudgington meant that new signing Steve Cherry was thrown in at the deep end against an Arsenal team who would finish fourth and lift the League Cup later that year. Tommy was the lone striker for much of the time, and he recalls that Arsenal were just too strong that day.

> *'It was a massive occasion and we took a big crowd to Highbury. It had been well hyped and I think we were hoping we could scrape a draw and bring them back to Home Park, but they just totally outclassed us that day.'*

Argyle followed the game at Highbury with a defeat against Reading, who were avenged for their earlier loss to the Greens at Elm Park on 7 February. Next they drew against Blackburn Rovers and lost against Sheffield United as their form ebbed away. A gap really began to open up between the pack and the top two teams.

Argyle eventually finished seventh in the Second Division that year, and it was their best stab at promotion to the top flight since 1962, when they came fifth, Wilf Carter and George Kirby scoring most of the goals. Derby County and Portsmouth were the teams promoted in the end. During the latter part of 1986 Argyle were near the top and if it had not been for a few silly slip-ups they could have experienced back-to-back promotions and could now be playing among the likes of Liverpool and Manchester United. Two defeats against Sunderland (who were relegated) and a couple of matches they should have won would have been enough to snatch second spot from Portsmouth and the fans would have finally been put out of their misery. Even if Argyle had finished bottom of the First Division the following season and been thumped by teams like Luton Town and Queen's Park Rangers, at least they would have been there. It is an attitude shared by many supporters today, as relegation from the Premiership brings a parachute payment of many millions of pounds and that kind of money can do wonders for a club.

However, it had been a decent showing for the Greens in their first season in the higher League, and Dave Smith and his men hoped they could improve on their League placing in the season ahead.

That same year Everton regained the League title from rivals Liverpool (their last to date), Arsenal won the League Cup and Coventry City won their first FA Cup, beating Spurs 3–2 in front of a crowd of 98,000. Manchester United and their new manager, Alex Ferguson, were in dire straits and in his column in the Argyle programme *My View*, dated 29 November 1986, Derek Henderson said 'Fergie would have to die in his office or resign to avoid the inevitable.' Full credit to United as they stuck by their man and eventually reaped the rewards. Their first League title was still seven years away, however, and they finished the 1986–87 season in 11th place in the top flight. Liverpool finished as runners-up to Everton, but the real surprise packages were Norwich City and Wimbledon, who finished fifth and sixth.

And what else was happening that year? Sheffield Wednesday finished just above Chelsea in 13th position as Leicester City, Manchester City and Aston Villa were all relegated from the top flight and bound for Home Park the following season. In Division Three Middlesbrough were rising, along with Harry Redknapp's Bournemouth, who were crowned League Champions, while Rotherham United could only manage 14th, one place lower than the Doncaster Rovers side Tommy was destined to end his professional career with. Newport County's slide into oblivion was gathering speed and they finished bottom and were relegated to Division Four. All of their stars had been sold and the end was nigh for the little Welsh team who had done so well and created that one brief moment in football history. They finished the season with just 37 points and conceded 86 goals as they stumbled towards their final season. In the Fourth Division, Swansea City, Torquay United and Lincoln City were unremarkable, but the Imps kept another of Tommy's future sides, Torquay, off the bottom and they were forced to apply for re-election as Lincoln fell into the Conference.

If the 1986–87 season was to be Argyle's swansong, then 1987–88 turned out to be a nightmare.

On 17 October Argyle managed to beat Leeds United 6–3 at Home Park. After going 10 games without a win, the sense of relief was evident on the faces of the players and the staff. Despite conceding two goals in seven minutes, Argyle grabbed all three points after Tommy got on the end of a cross and unleashed a last-minute screamer. The win moved them away from the danger zone and they ambled along for a while longer.

Despite Smith's optimism, Argyle finished in 16th position and just 10 points away from the relegation zone, even though they had added players like Nicky Marker, Dougie Anderson and Mark Smith to the mix. There was not a lot for the fans to get excited about but Tommy, who was by now 32 years old, was still banging the goals in. He finished the season with 26 from 48 matches. One of his best performances came on 12 September 1987 when Argyle drew 3–3 with West Bromwich Albion in the rain and mud. It was an average game until the 70th minute when the match just exploded. Anderson lobbed an ambitious shot goalwards from the wing and Tommy's jack-in-the-box leap over the defenders ended with him scoring a magnificent goal. Ron Atkinson's team had been one up until then, and three minutes later John Clayton made it 2–1 to the Greens as he was just about to be substituted. Albion's George Reilly (the same man whose goal had knocked Argyle out of the FA Cup semi-final) had a penalty saved in the 80th minute and Carlton

Palmer's hesitancy let Tommy in for Argyle's third. In a split second he had dribbled past two defenders, turned towards goal and stabbed the ball home to make it 3–1. Unfortunately, Argyle could not hold on and it was 3–2 within a couple of minutes. With the last kick of the game, a West Brom set piece found Carlton Palmer's head and the Baggies rescued a point.

Plymouth battled on and the 1988–89 season was another struggle against relegation. The highlight for Tommy was his four League goals against Blackburn Rovers in a 4–3 win on 5 November 1988. He bagged his 100th League goal for the Greens along the way. The ball had gone out of the ground towards the end of the match, seemingly lost forever, so Tommy was surprised when somebody handed it into the offices of *The Evening Herald* and he got to keep it. He had received a standing ovation earlier in the season when he scored a hat-trick against Stoke City and recalls playing some of the best football in his life that day. There were games and goals that lay ahead and Tommy was enjoying terrifying defences week in and week out, although he knew he was nearing the end of his playing days. He was rapidly approaching his 33rd birthday but still felt he had a couple of good seasons left in him. His performances on the park certainly suggested this and new manager Ken Brown's team were struggling just as Smith's had done the season before. They finished in 18th position and any doubters were soon silenced as Tommy finished with 26 goals from 54 appearances, keeping them from relegation. Maybe he had lost a yard of pace, but his game was not just about running. His technical ability, coupled with his intelligence, found him in the right position at the right time and he scored over a third of the goals for Argyle that season. Now considered a veteran, he was safe in the knowledge that he had written his name into the history books and in the process had become a legend to the Home Park faithful.

Tommy will never forget his last season at Argyle. Ken Brown's men started the campaign with a prestigious friendly against

Brazilian side Botafogo, who boasted players from the national team such as Josimar, Mauro Galvao and Delei. Out of the 26 League matches Tommy played that season under Brown, they managed to win just eight and Tommy found the net on 10 occasions. Arsenal had turned them over again, 8–1 over two legs, in the League Cup second round. Tommy was sick of the sight of the Gunners. Oxford United knocked them out of the FA Cup in the third round, but he had still managed to score three from the five Cup matches he had been involved in. Ken Brown's last game turned out to be against Wolverhampton Wanderers on 3 March when the Greens lost 1–0 at home and were booed off the pitch. It was Argyle's ninth game without a win and relegation was a serious possibility. There had been a few glimmers of sunshine along the way for Tommy, but the pressure was really on the 34-year-old to perform and score goals week after week to keep them out of the relegation zone.

After giving it a lot of consideration, Tommy applied for the vacant manager's post and was interviewed by Stuart Dawe and the Argyle board. Players like Kenny Dalglish had succeeded as player-manager, and although Tommy realised it would not be easy, he was confident he could manage the club. However, he was turned down and was told by Dawe that they were looking for an established manager and could not afford to take a risk on someone who was unproven due to their precarious League position. The man they were looking for had to have a track record of success in management, and despite all the things Tommy had achieved in the game he had no managerial experience. He realised this was a fair point, as with two months of the season left they had to get results quickly, and there could be no bedding-in time for the incoming manager. Whoever came in would have to be able to cope with life at the bottom end of the Division. As Dawe and his board had said that they were not willing to employ an ex-player with no experience (like they had done with John Hore), when they finally unveiled ex-player Dave Kemp as the new manager Tommy was not amused.

> *'I don't know why I didn't get a look in – maybe they just didn't want a player-manager. I was just a bit bewildered when they took an ex-player on after they told me they were looking for someone more experienced.'*

Argyle was Kemp's first managerial job and what he was about to do to the team was not pretty to watch.

The long-ball game had first been played under Dave Smith, but he was not a purist, he liked to add a bit of spice to the mix, although he did tell his defenders to thump the ball into the final third of the pitch when they had possession. It is not a very creative way of playing, but it can be effective, and Argyle needed points quickly. The long-ball game is all about statistics and regaining possession; when a player gets the ball he needs to get it up front into the opposition's half as soon as possible. This is usually done by thumping it to the forwards which therefore cuts out the football played in the middle of the pitch. Indeed, a midfielder is not really needed, all that is required is some big defenders to make headers in their own half or in the middle third and get the ball up front. By keeping the ball in the air and whacking it forward, the law of averages suggests you are going to create opportunities. It is a style first played by Wimbledon and was highly successful for the Dons as they climbed from the Fourth Division to the top, winning the FA Cup along the way. Dave Kemp had been part of the Wimbledon coaching staff and the Argyle board saw him, and his grasp of the long-ball game, as a quick fix to their problems.

When Dave Kemp took over, Argyle were in the bottom four and straight away he implemented his new tactics. His first match was against Sunderland on 3 March 1990 and Tommy scored twice in a 3–0 win against a side that went on to win the Play-offs that year. A few days before the match, Kemp sat in the changing rooms with the players and told them that he would have to make drastic changes to their play to get them out of trouble. If they played the Wimbledon system they would do better than most teams, and it did not really matter what type of players they had, just as long as they played the system they would have a reasonable amount of success. It was against everything Tommy had been taught; Shankly's vision of pass and move, Jack Charlton's tactical prowess and Len Ashurst's physical game. Such managers would never have endorsed such a doctrine. Watching long-ball football evokes moans and groans from the crowd as another ball is thumped aimlessly in the air in the hope that somebody will get their boot on the end of it. Hit and hope football had Tommy, who was captain by this time, less than impressed.

Chapter 19
Faulty Towers

Despite all of the goings-on, Kemp did enough to get Argyle out of hot water and they finished in 16th position, a slight improvement on the season before. Under Kemp Tommy played 16 League matches and they won five and drew six as he added another five goals, ending the season with 18. His last goal for the Greens came on 21 April 1990 as Argyle drew 1–1 with Newcastle United at Home Park, and his final appearance in a green shirt came in a 0–0 draw against Watford on 28 April 1990, the penultimate game of the season, as Tommy, to his surprise, missed out on the last game at Bradford City. There is a common misconception that Tommy and Dave Kemp fell out, but this was not the case:

> 'Before the last match, Kempy asked me if I thought Owen Pickard was good enough for the first team; he had been scoring a lot of goals in the reserves and when I said I thought the lad deserved a chance, he never told me he would be playing Pickard in my place, and that hurt. I never played for Argyle again and it would have been nice to bow out in front of the fans even if the game was away.'

It had all changed for the worse for Tommy when Argyle hired a coach called Alan Gillett. He had worked for the FA but never played the game professionally. He immediately took a dislike to Tommy and his arrival spelled the end for him. Even though Tommy had scored 18 goals that year, Gillett did not believe he was capable of scoring any more, despite the fact that Kemp thought Tommy was still their best player, which he told new signing Danis

Salman a few months earlier when Argyle were really struggling. Tommy says that the situation…

> *'…was all a bit political, but Gillett was definitely pulling the strings. He had never played or managed at professional level so it's strange how he had such a big influence. I was no spring chicken I know, but I still had goals left in me.'*

To add insult to injury, Tommy was never told he was going to be released by Argyle at the end of the season. The man who had been voted Player of the Year three times, won the Golden Boot, played in the semi-final, scored four against Blackburn, received standing ovations and scored 10 goals in nine games as Argyle won promotion was not granted the respect he deserved as his employers failed to tell him he was no longer required. Instead, Plymouth Argyle's greatest centre-forward had to learn of his release from a local newspaper:

> *'People think that me and Dave Kemp fell out but that is not true. I just think it was pretty shabby how they got rid of me; nobody at the club had the courage to tell me I had been released.'*

The following season, after his departure from Home Park, Tommy bumped into Robbie Turner, who was playing up front for Argyle and having a very frustrating time. He told Tommy that since he had left he was sick of hearing his name and that he was just the type of player Argyle needed. Turner believed Tommy would have scored a bagful if he had not been released. He said he spent all of his time knocking balls into the box, bashing people about and creating chances for Argyle, but the problem was that nobody was there to get on the end of those chances. In the end Kemp signed

Keith Edwards from Oldham Athletic, who was a similar player to Tommy but he did not have anything like the same impact.

Tommy rarely ponders his exit from Home Park, but there will always be a part of him that feels a little hurt by the actions of some of the coaching staff at the time. Thankfully, at such a late stage in his career he had developed a thick skin; some of the biggest names in football had tried to give him a bit of stick over the years and the steely determination and icy resolve of those like Bill Shankly and Len Ashurst must have rubbed off on him. Tommy had learned from the Norman Hunter episode and in the end it had been the Leeds United legend who had egg on his face. Such farcical episodes were part and parcel of the professional game, but not one to be walked over, Tommy fought his corner on numerous occasions. He had grown to love Plymouth Argyle and had become the club's star striker. Tommy was there with them through the highs and the lows, giving it his all and it has been appreciated. He has shared all of the emotions on those wet nights and sunny afternoons when a flick of the ball or a clever trick could provide the fans with what they craved. Those flashes of inspiration or snap goals in the dying seconds beneath the floodlights have bound him to the fans of Plymouth Argyle forever. Whenever he returns to Home Park he receives a warm greeting from those whose loyalty serves as an unending 'thank you' for past service and they will keep his name alive on the terraces forever.

Perhaps he could have played on for the Greens for a little while longer, but by the time he collected his things from Home Park and said goodbye, he knew he had done his bit for the club. In his last season at Home Park Tommy was top scorer once again and his departure cost Argyle dearly the following season. It was a typical case of politics over football and, as they slipped out of what is now the Championship in 1992, they managed just 42 goals, a far cry from the halcyon days of the mid-to-late 1980s when Tommy Tynan was regularly scoring 20 goals or more a season. Murderous clouds would soon be looming in the skies over Home Park and a struggle for power threatened Plymouth Argyle's very existence as incoming club owner Dan McCauley flexed his muscles. The quaint little Devon club were soon be facing a struggle for survival. In their first season without Tommy signs of what was to come began to show, with poor peformances in the League and particularly in front of goal.

After his departure from Argyle and Dundee, Dave Smith had taken over at Torquay United and was soon making the most of it. He had managed to get the team into shape and he wanted Tommy on board. When the end came for him at Plymouth, Smith offered him a player-coach role. This was an ideal introduction into coaching for the veteran striker and they soon came to an agreement on a contract. Tommy still wanted to be a player rather than a coach, and some of his duties were shared to allow him enough time to concentrate on his game. For example, he would take a session on striking the ball or positioning, but he still wanted to feel like a member of the team so assistants would come in early and do the setting up and some of the office-based stuff, leaving Tommy to get on with the football side of things. It was a nice arrangement and it worked for quite a while.

Torquay United started the 1990–91 campaign in great form. Like at many of the smaller clubs there was not a great deal of money or talent around, and squads were small and full of 'grafters' who could do a decent job as part of a team. Torquay's early results took them straight to the top of the table and things were looking good until they were struck down with some serious injuries. Five or six of the first team were out of action, and with no back up Torquay were soon relying on the youngsters. Despite their best efforts, the results started to dry up and the descent began. Unfortunately, not all of Dave Smith's backroom staff were on his side and as soon as things started to go wrong, the knives were out. The rot started right at the top and Smith ultimately paid the price for United's misfortune. There were a few who benefitted from his departure, but Tommy was not one of them. His loyalty to Smith was without question and it was a pity there were not a few more people in the boardroom and on the coaching staff who could have fought Smith's corner instead of fanning the flames. John Impey was appointed as Dave Smith's successor, but in all fairness he could have done more to keep Smith in his job.

Maybe Tommy should have seen the signs at the very beginning. After he had talked about money with Dave Smith, he went to see the chairman, Mike Bateson. Bateson held the belief that footballers should not even be on a contract, and if they were unable to work then they should go on the sick. His expertise leaned more towards selling UPVC windows than running a professional football team. You cannot knock him when it comes to selling windows as that is how he made his money, but running a football club requires a little more refinement, coupled with complex negotiating skills and tactical knowledge. In his defence, he has kept Torquay alive for all of these years and they still exist largely due to him. When Tommy's signing fee was £400 short, Bateson wrote out a cheque in front of him and gave it to him there and then.

This seemed to change when Torquay were 15 points clear at the top of the League, with Tommy scoring goals, which was followed by a series of controversies that led to him being fined two weeks' wages and put up before the FA. The first incident occurred after Tommy had heard that John Impey, the Torquay youth coach, had spoken to Dave Smith and told him that Tommy was finished in the game and he would not able to score any more goals. When he netted a couple of goals in the very next match, Tommy made his point by sliding across the pitch on his knees and giving the board a two-fingered salute. He received a fine of two weeks' wages for the gesture, but Tommy felt that it was worth it.

A second incident occured in a hotel room where some of the senior players were playing a game of cards:

'After a few beers, things got a little bit heated. I was trying to stop a fight and Wes Saunders ended up punching me and giving me a black eye. Later, I went to Saunders's room to try and have it out with him. Unfortunately, things got a little bit heated once again and it turned into a brawl. We had had a drink and I ended up picking up the nearest thing, which was a kettle, and I whacked him with it. The disciplinary was set up by Bateson on the Monday and it was a joke, he hadn't even told the PFA what was going on. He literally told me that I wasn't going to be playing for the club again. It was so one-sided it was untrue. The next thing I know, people are telling me they've seen Impey driving around Torquay in the chairman's Rolls-Royce and after Dave Smith was sacked, they gave him the job. I felt sorry for Dave and I've got a lot of time for him but that is the only time he let me down. He didn't say a word during the disciplinary and I just felt he could have stuck up for me. Years later, I bumped into him in Plymouth town centre and he said that one day he would tell me what really went on, but I never heard from him and it's so long ago now, who cares…?'

The incident which soured the milk still further occurred when Bateson put a stop on players getting a couple of complimentary tickets for family and friends. As player-coach Tommy felt it was only right that he stood up for the players, after all Plainmoor was not packed to the rafters every game, but Bateson was not happy about Tommy's intervention. Nevertheless, Tommy felt it was his duty and unfortunately it only led to more ill-feeling.

The final incident which marked not only the start of Torquay's slump but also the end of Tommy's time at the club occurred just after the board appointed John Impey as Dave Smith's successor, which came on the back of Tommy's disciplinary hearing. Tommy told him that he believed he had been stabbing Smith in the back for months and that he had done absolutely nothing to help him keep his job. Before Tommy knew what was happening, Impey had him training and playing with the reserves. Impey was just trying to make a point, but Tommy was 35 years old and was not one to be pushed around.

As the mood around Plainmoor soured, the club's 15 point margin started to disappear. Tommy then found out that the chairman and the board had prepared a retainer list of every player that they were going to keep the following season. Despite being the leading scorer in the League at the time, prior to his demotion to the reserves, Tommy was surprised to learn that he was not on the list, and he was not impressed. When Ken Furphy interviewed Tommy for the radio, Torquay's margin at the top had been reduced to just four points. With a team packed full of inexperienced youngsters, they were being found out on the pitch and exploited. Furphy could not believe that Tommy's name was not on the retainer list and that the Torquay board had gone public with it.

Torquay's poor run of results, coupled with multiple injuries to first-team players, led to Tommy being called in for a word with the men upstairs. In a meeting with two of the directors and John Impey Tommy was told that he had to prove to them that he could still score goals. As top scorer for the club he told them he did not have to prove anything, and Impey accused him of being arrogant. Maybe it was arrogance, but as long as he could back it up, who cared? Nevertheless, the meeting led to Tommy being back on the fringes of the first team once more.

Despite all of the commotion, Torquay finished the season facing a Play-off Final against Blackpool and Tommy looked forward to playing at Wembley for the very first time. His wife Elaine was up to see the game with current Argyle chairman Paul Stapleton and his wife Kim. Tommy was hoping to put on a good show in his last appearance for Torquay. When Elaine and the Stapletons drove up to Wembley before the kick-off, they were surprised to see Tommy stood outside in his tracksuit with his kit bag. Bateson and company were proving a point once more, however, and they had left it right to the last minute to omit Tommy from the squad. They even made him travel with the team when they had no intention of picking him – it was an underhanded thing to do and Tommy never did play at Wembley. Instead, the Tynans and the Stapletons went into London for a few drinks and did not even bother to watch the game, which Torquay won, gaining promotion for the first time in 26 seasons. It turned out that on the morning of the match Tommy's apprentice had been told to clear his kit away as he would not be playing. Tommy then went and asked Bateson and Impey why they had brought him if they had no intention of letting him play, and neither of them could look him in the eye. When they returned to Torquay's hotel after the match, Elaine bumped into Bateson who acted like nothing had happened and that they were all the best of friends. She took great delight in telling him exactly what she thought of him.

And then, in the blink of an eye, it was all over. It had been a career that had lasted 19 years and had accumulated 258 goals in 650 matches. Even today Tommy is widely regarded as one of the best centre-forwards never to play in the top flight, and as we sit nursing our pints, he talks quite candidly about his playing days. I can see the gleam in his eye which accompanies that knowing smile as we talk about everything he has done in the game. He is proud to have played his part in Shankly and Paisley's world-class set-up, even if he did not quite reach the pinnacle with Liverpool. For as long as football is played, people will know of those Liverpool teams and the influence they have had on the evolution of the game. From the fans right down to the men who swept the floors at Anfield, everyone played their part. Tommy can describe to you the stains on the walls of the boot room and the heady smells and crazy nights at Anfield that will be gone forever when they relocate. He scored a shedload throughout the ranks and won numerous youth awards and that is something he is, and should rightly be, proud of. After Liverpool, wherever he went he scored and he rubbed shoulders with some of the greats of the game along the way.

After all the nonsense at Torquay, which is in no way reflected on the fans who Tommy describes as absolutely brilliant, he continued playing for a little while longer. He had a brief spell at Doncaster Rovers, until they paid up the contracts of all the senior professionals, and he had a little venture into non-League football when he took over as player-manager of Goole Town for a couple of months. After that he played locally for a couple of Sheffield teams as the Tynans settled back in Sheffield. Soon the calling would come and Tommy Tynan would return to Plymouth in their darkest hour.

'It was a shame what happened at the end of my career both at Argyle and at Torquay. At Torquay, I knew I was coming to the end of my career. I was scoring goals, doing a bit of coaching and enjoying myself in the beginning. Unfortunately, there were too many people with agendas. The football was supposed to be the most important thing, but what the Torquay baord called professionalism I thought was laughable. It was a bit of a shame really.'

Chapter 20
Murderous Clouds

After football and back in Sheffield, alongside his wife, Tommy ran a couple of pubs. But back in Plymouth the 1990s were a time of terrible instability for the club Tommy had loved playing for so much. When Tommy left the side at the end of the 1989–90 season they had finished 16th in what is now the Championship. At the beginning of the 1990s Dan McCauley bought the club and things got a great deal worse. During his reign, which started in early 1990 and lasted until current chairman Paul Stapleton and his consortium bought McCauley out in August 2001, seven men took the manager's seat as the club lurched from one crisis to another. At the end of the 1991–92 season Argyle lost their Championship status. Three years later they were relegated to the bottom tier for the first time in their history.

Of course, McCauley was not all bad and, although he liked to be in control and to know exactly what was going on, he was a pretty down-to-earth guy. He could also be extremely generous, as Tommy remembers:

> 'Dan wasn't all bad and, don't forget, I lost a lot because of him so I'm trying to show both sides of the coin. There was a time when players' wages were not paid and I think he took about £200,000 out of his own personal account and paid them. Also, when Gordon Ward, who used to run the Far Post Club, died, Dan gave his wife a cheque for about £25,000 to see her through but I'm not sure if she took it or not.'

After relegation to Division Three (now League Two) in May 1995, Neil Warnock was brought in to steady the ship. Twelve months later Ronnie Mauge scored the only goal in a 1–0 win at Wembley against Darlington in the Play-off Final and Argyle were promoted at the first attempt. It was their second go at the Play-offs: Peter Shilton's side had been beaten by Burnley in the Second Division Play-off semi-final two seasons earlier. Warnock took them back up, and after the 1996–97 campaign in the Second Division (now called League One) they finished in 19th place. The 1997–98 season started disastrously, and by then Warnock had left the club and his assistant Mick Jones was in charge. On 9 September Argyle beat Walsall 2–1 in their ninth League match of the season and recorded their first win of the campaign. By Christmas they had played 25 matches, recorded five wins and picked up just 25 points. Relegation to the basement division called once again and they finally finished third from bottom and were relegated alongside Southend United, Carlisle United and Brentford.

Argyle's first win on 9 September took their tally of League goals from the first nine games to a paltry nine. That night the local newspaper, *The Evening Herald,* ran a story on the back page about the proposed Tradium project. The council had not heard from Dan McCauley over their plans to redevelop the Home Park site. They had been trying to hold discussions with him about the £27 million project without success so they had decided to go ahead with things 'with or without him'. By this time McCauley was not a happy man. Results had been so bad that the supporters were naturally unhappy and they voiced their opinions. They had booed the players off the pitch, they had jeered at the manager and at the chairman and his wife. Unfortunately, it appeared as though Dan was unable to take the insults on the chin and had taken it personally. In retaliation he threatened to put the club up for sale with an inflated asking price of £3 million and he wrote to the Football League to tell them of his intentions to resign from the League at the end of the season. To add insult to injury, he had gone to the Press threatening to build a supermarket on Home Park, as he did not believe he would find a buyer for the club in the nine months before the end of the season and was planning to dissolve the football team and redevelop the site if a buyer could not be found. Suddenly, the knives were out. The man may have been a multi-millionaire, but he was messing with 111 years of tradition and something which many Plymothians held close to their hearts. Plymouth City Council spokesman Ian Blackstone was quick to reply to McCauley's threats, stating that he would be unlikely to get planning permission to build a supermarket on the site and so the war of words raged on.

On 10 September Nottingham-based millionaire businessman Sandy Anderson gave the Argyle faithful a ray of hope in an otherwise gloomy time for the club. He told the newspaper that he may buy the club if a venture he was involved in to buy a Premier League side fell through. Anderson had failed in his bid to buy Nottingham Forest in January 1997 and his consortium were now attempting to buy an unnamed side. Anderson declined to comment on just how much he felt Argyle was worth, and nothing more was heard from him as the situation went from bad to worse. Legal experts had confirmed that McCauley could close Argyle down at the end of the season if he wanted to. As a major shareholder he could put the club into voluntary liquidation, but he would have to pay up all of the contracts of the staff and players, which would not even start to put a dent in his wealth.

In trying to present a balanced view of the situation it is fair to say that there were a lot of people gunning for McCauley, but he certainly helped to fan the flames. As club chairman he would have been wise to ignore the comments of the fans; there is not a club in the land whose management and board of directors have not come under attack when what is being served up on the pitch is dire. Perhaps there was a better way of handling the situation; for example, maybe a couple of loan signings could have been brought in to try and improve the situation on the pitch or the McCauleys could have simply stayed away from Home Park. It is all conjecture now, but Tommy believes that Dan made it a lot worse for himself and his wife by going to the Press:

> *'What happened to Dan was bad but all chairmen get stick from the fans when it goes wrong. By making the comments that he made to the Press he made himself a target and a figure of hatred, it couldn't have been an easy time for him. The McCauleys even received a death-threat from one deluded fan, so that must have been hell to live with. I remember there was some police chief or some kind of high-up copper in the Devon and Cornwall Constabulary who told Dan that they could not guarantee his and his wife's safety in Devon and Cornwall.'*

At the same time as McCauley went to the Press, he was also criticising *The Evening Herald*. He was unhappy with what he believed was 'biased' reporting and he banned the newspaper from the ground and from speaking to manager Mick Jones, his assistant Kevin Blackwell and to any of the players, telling them that disciplinary action would be taken if they disobeyed him. The newspaper was quick to hit back at McCauley, saying that they believed it was the fans who were the victims in this argument and they would not be silenced. They were quick to point out that this was not a personal attack on Dan McCauley and that they had offered to meet with him to talk and to give him the chance to explain to the fans exactly what was going on, but McCauley had quickly refused the offer. At this point it looked like he had raised the drawbridge and manned the battlements in preparation as he told the fans that he would not be spending another penny on the team.

It was not over yet; bad news was coming thick and fast. On Thursday 11 September safety experts gave the club until Saturday to do repairs to Home Park or part of the ground would be closed down.

There were problems with the CCTV system, and strengthening to the safety barrier in the family area had to be carried out. Several months earlier, part of the ground was closed and the capacity was reduced to 9,975 because the PA system was inadequate.

After a couple of years away, Tommy and his family returned to Plymouth in early 1997 to run the Golden Hind pub in Mannamead. Now in his early 40s, he had been out of football for a number of years, although he still did various interviews and media work when required. He followed the developments at Home Park with great interest and was saddened and shocked that the club he had so many fantastic memories of could soon be facing extinction. One night, out of the blue, he received a telephone call and was informed that there was a group of businessmen who were interested in a possible buyout of Argyle and they wanted to know if they could use him as the frontman.

On 12 September Plymouth City Council launched its own bid to find a buyer for the club after talks with McCauley the previous evening had broken down. They stated that:

> *'It is obvious that McCauley wants out and we will not be extending the current lease and we will not let him build a supermarket on the Home Park site.'*

At the same time *The Evening Herald* announced that a group of businessmen, who wanted to keep their identities secret at that point, were interested in buying the club. Tommy did a piece in the paper after being asked to be the frontman:

> *'They wanted to see what the fans' reaction would be before making their next move. They came to me because they knew that the fans knew me and they appreciated what I had done for the club on the pitch.'*

At the same time the consortium had been in touch with Plymouth Argyle's Supporters and Training Development Trust and they had assured them they had the best interests of the club and its supporters at heart. When the news broke, Tommy was surprised to hear that Dan McCauley and chief executive Roger Matthews had called in at his pub. He was out with Elaine at the time:

> *'I was informed that Dan and Roger had come into the pub, but I have no idea why they came in when they could have just picked up the phone if they wanted to talk to me. I had only ever met Dan on one occasion at that point so I really had no idea why he came in. Apparently, while he was in my pub they were approached by a reporter and Matthews said Dan was in Plymouth for other business and he decided to come into the pub for a half.'*

While all of this was going on off the pitch, Mick Jones was struggling to find 14 fit players. On Monday 15 September *The Evening Herald* ran an article entitled *'Fans Come First'* and warned Dan that he was playing a dangerous game. They also showed pictures of a crane they had hired in which reporter Chris Errington had climbed to defy McCauley, after the newspaper was banned from the ground. It was a masterstroke, and the paper continued to report and take pictures of the Argyle matches. It was at this time that Tommy released a Press statement telling the public that the consortium had appointed a solicitor and an accountant and were preparing to make a bid; the crucial meeting was to take place on Thursday 18 September. It was then that St Austell insurance broker Clive Rosevear and Russell Peak, a company director from Liskeard, were linked to the consortium, along with former Argyle directors Dennis Angilley and Graham Jasper. In a statement, Tommy said:

'It is not taking place until then [the Thursday meeting] because certain people are not in the country at the minute. The response from the fans has been good and my phone has not stopped ringing with people wanting to make donations. There are three avenues they [the consortium] could go down and they will decide which one to take. Once this is all out my job is done. I will help them as much as I can but at the end of the day they are the ones with the money.'

Tommy was amazed at the reaction of people wanting to donate. The news that there was a major player interested had cheered everyone up. Among the many donations Tommy received, one of the most heart-warming came from a builder in North Prospect who sent him a cheque for quite a few thousand pounds. He also remembers being stopped in the street by a little old lady who told him she would send him what she could when she got her pension. In total, around £1 million was raised. Many fans had been staying away from Home Park in protest of McCauley but, despite their dreadful form at the time and the fact that all of this must have been affecting them, none of the antics off the pitch had anything to do with manager Mick Jones or his players; the newspaper urged fans to get behind the team and start coming back through the turnstiles. On 16 September *The Evening Herald* launched a campaign to save Argyle:

'Yesterday McCauley carried out his threat and laid off commercial manager Donna Shirley and three other employees.'

On Wednesday 17 September the PFA got involved. Gordon Taylor said that Argyle were wrong to gag players and gave them permission to talk to the Press. Taylor also said that McCauley could not take action against the players as long as they did not bring the game into disrepute. If players wanted to be interviewed about a match then they could and they would not be charged. At the same time local celebrities such as the Olympic swimmer Sharon Davies and former England goalkeeper Nigel Martyn were lending their support to *The Evening Herald's* campaign to save Plymouth Argyle.

Late on Thursday 18 September Tommy released a statement to the Press which was printed in the paper the very next day. 'Pilgrims for the People' set out an eight-point plan, while at the time the consortium's identities were still kept secret. It can now be revealed that a rich American businessman called Albert Scardino was behind it, and he was willing to put up half the money needed to buy McCauley out if the fans could show their commitment to the cause and raise the other half.

Pilgrims for the People eight-point plan:

- *A sound financial backing and management structure.*

- *Committed board of directors who hold Argyle's interests above everything else.*

- *To elect a supporter to the board.*

- *Strong progressive commercial department to establish lasting partnerships with business and the community.*

- *Opportunities for fans to buy shares in the club.*

- *Constructive discussion with Plymouth City Council over the Tradium project.*

- *Realistic investment in the team.*

- *Strong and permanent youth development programme.*

The plan was devised after the consortium had been in consultation with many experts and a city solicitor who had experience in football club buyouts. Unfortunately, it never came to fruition and Dan McCauley backed down from his plan to wind the club up at the end of the season, releasing the following statement to the Press:

> *'It's time to lift the gloom at the club and say that Plymouth Argyle will live beyond this season. I will be writing to the Football League in the next couple of days advising them of that. At least this will lift the fear off people's minds. Football means so much to me and I just couldn't let this club die.'*

Argyle sauntered along for another few seasons in the basement division and Scardino eventually bought Notts County. McCauley said he never received an official approach from the consortium. Tommy had done his bit for the Greens. In 1998 Paul Stapleton became a director and a consortium led by him eventually bought Argyle in August 2001. It is interesting to look at the 'Pilgrims for the People' plan today. All of the eight points have been achieved under the leadership of Stapleton. Argyle managed to buy the lease from the city council and the development of the South Stand is the last piece in the jigsaw.

Today, Argyle proudly sit in the Championship and things look good for the club who, under the current manager Paul Sturrock, achieved two promotions in as many years. After 'Pilgrims for the People', Tommy became the commercial manager of the club, while McCauley was still at the controls and, unfortunately for him,

McCauley became another in a long line of high-profile figures who tried to interfere in Tommy's affairs:

'The Scardino thing was looking good for a while and there were quite a few people who wanted Dan out of the club. We went to the first meeting and what was said was good. They were talking about setting up a shares issue and Scardino was interested, although he had not committed himself, he was just listening to what everyone had to say, but he was definitely a 'maybe.' He could see that there was a lot of potential if it could be done correctly. And then, all of a sudden, he dropped out for no reason and it may well have been that Dan had been leaning on a few people and scared him off. After it was all over Dan tried to make a bit of peace, and he certainly wasn't as vocal as he had been before. That's when he offered me the job as commercial manager, but I had still only met him twice at that time. I don't think he liked me because I was more famous than him. He certainly had a passion for football, but he wasn't an Argyle fanatic. Roger Matthews had to fax all newspaper articles and information to him so he was certainly well informed and knew how people felt. Why I was sacked as commercial manager is anybody's guess. Peter Bloom even came to me at Christmas and said, "You've sold 90 per cent of the advertising boards, boxes and committee rooms," and it was the first time they had made a profit. The problem I had after losing my job was to do with finance. I already had the Stoke Social Club and I was set to buy the Far Post Club based on my earnings from that and what I earned in my role as commercial manager. Dan then pulled the plug, saying running the Far Post and being commercial manager was a conflict of interests, and he didn't even have the balls to tell me himself. The irony of it is that the next commercial manager owned three pubs!'

It is fair to say that Tommy lost everything over that venture. Sadly, the game was never to make him rich (he was from that generation of footballers who just missed out on the massive influx of cash) but he did make enough to give him and his family a comfortable standard of living. He feels privileged to have been able to make a career out of something he loved doing. It could easily have been different, he could just as easily spent his life working in the docks, lugging boxes on Scottie Road or doing back-breaking shifts in factories across Merseyside as the city council edged ever closer towards bankruptcy. Tommy was one of the lucky ones, virtually no one escaped from the streets of the council estates, the tenements and dilapidated boarding houses which made up many parts of Liverpool at the time. Sport and music were the only escapes; everyone wanted to start a band, get a part in a movie or become a footballer. George Best had glamourised the image of the footballer in the 1960s with his hedonistic lifestyle but it would take another 30 years for those involved in the game to become mega-rich from their craft. In defining football as a craft, we can also see it as an art form; many people have likened a slinky run down the wing or a magnificent goal to poetry in motion. If art and sport can be defined as the ultimate forms of expression, when we look back at the career of Tommy Tynan is there any one of us who would not have liked to do what he did in the game?

At 53, he still finds time to write his Thursday column for *The Evening Herald* called *Upfront with Tommy*, as well as playing for the Argyle veterans and driving his taxicab around Plymouth. He is always quick to reply when people ask him why he drives a cab:

'They say to me, "Tommy, why the hell are you driving a cab?" One of the reasons is I can please myself, I'm my own boss and I meet all sorts of interesting people along the way. Maybe one or two of them might try to take the mickey but how many of them have seen what

I have seen, met the people I have met and done what I have done in their lives? I was a generation too early and missed out on the big money, but it's interesting to wonder how much some of the players I played with would be worth today. Take people like Gordon Nisbet, Leigh Cooper, Kevin Hodges, Garry Nelson and Gerry McElhinney, they would get into any side in the Championship at least. Today I don't think that there is the same quality of home-grown players coming from the lower Leagues as there was when I was playing. I can understand that the top teams get the best players in the world and many of them are from other countries, but I don't think it's about football anymore, it's all about money and I think we have lost something because of that. It's been taken away from the grass roots. You look at the youngsters at top teams such as Arsenal. They spend a couple of million quid on a 16 or 17-year-old from France or Italy rather than investing in British players. Today at 18 you can sign a three or four-year contract and be made for life, back then I think you worked harder for it. Dear old Bill Shankly would be turning in his grave. Still, that, as they say, is progress I suppose...'

Epilogue

29 April 2008: Home Park – Mickey Evans's testimonial

Fellow Argyle legend Mickey Evans retired in 2006 and his testimonial happened on 29 April 2008 and it was only fitting that Argyle's greatest player got a run out in front of a new green generation. When he stepped out onto the Home Park pitch the crowd treated Tommy in a familiar fashion. The testimonial was a chance for Tommy to be with some of the current squad, as well as some of the old boys, and running out onto the pitch brought back memories and seemed a fitting moment to draw a conclusion to the story of a boy who defied the odds, and the factories and the warehouses of Liverpool, to become a professional footballer and a prolific goalscorer. Watching him out there on the turf that night felt like I had stepped back in time and I could not help scanning the crowd for the old dear with the brolly now long gone, or the bloke that used to stand behind us smoking roll-up cigarettes from beginning to end.

At 52, Tommy's appearance was a token gesture to Mickey Evans, who was worried about giving him a full 90 minutes because he wanted to win the game! It was nice to see that the crowd had not forgotten what Tommy had done for them over the years and they greeted him with a cheer, as little boys looked up at their fathers wondering who it was they were cheering and why he was wearing the green and white.

'That's Tommy Tynan, the greatest Argyle player of them all,' said the bloke beside me to his son as he sat clutching his programme.

Tommy's statistics

(League, League Cup, FA Cup and Cup-Winners' Cup)

Team	Total Apps	Goals
Liverpool	0	0
Swansea City (loan)	6	2
Sheffield Wednesday	91	31
Lincoln City	9	1
Newport County	266	88
Plymouth Argyle	302	136
Rotherham United	32	13
Torquay United	35	13
Doncaster Rovers	11	1
Total	**752**	**285**

ND - #0303 - 270225 - C0 - 234/156/12 - PB - 9781780914107 - Gloss Lamination